The
BRECON & MERTHYR RAILWAY

by
D.S.M. Barrie O.B.E.

revised by
R.W. Kidner

THE OAKWOOD PRESS

First edition 1964
Reprinted 1973, 1975, 1980
Second enlarged edition 1991

© Oakwood Press 1991

ISBN 0 85361 410 5

Typeset by Gem Publishing Company, Brightwell, Wallingford, Oxfordshire.

Printed by Alpha Print Ltd, Witney, Oxfordshire.

Acknowledgments

For the original work in 1957, and subsequent editions, the author received much help from a number of noted railway historians, many of whom are unfortunately no longer with us. They included: C.R. Clinker, G.W.T. Daniel, A.T. Davies, F.K. Davies, George Dow, J.M. Dunn, M.D. Greville, Charles Hadfield, V.S. Haram, T.L. Jones, W. Jones, C. Judge, Charles E. Lee, John Murray, H.W. Parr, A.J. Pritchard, R.C. Riley, R.M. Robbins, T.B. Sands, W.J. Thomas and E.R. Mountford.

He also acknowledged his gratitude to John de Winton of Brecon, great-grandson of the company's first Chairman, for the loan of material relating to the period 1855–75, and to R.E. Thomas for help in making up the loco-motive list.

For this enlarged edition, special thanks are due to the National Library of Wales for making maps and other documents available; Mr I.J. Williams, Mr H.E. Williams, the late F.E. Howard, British Rail, Western Region, the Brecon Mountain Railway, Mr C.P. Pickford, Mr W.W. Tasker, Mr C.J.W. Powell, and Mr T. McCarthy.

Published by
The OAKWOOD PRESS
P.O.Box 122, Headington, Oxford.

Contents

	Introduction	5
Chapter One	A Railway of Character	7
Chapter Two	The Beginning	13
Chapter Three	Completion to Merthyr	25
Chapter Four	Brecon Joint Station	27
Chapter Five	Looking Southwards	31
Chapter Six	Fighting the LNWR	39
Chapter Seven	The Pontypridd, Caerphilly & Newport Railway	43
Chapter Eight	Modest Prosperity	47
Chapter Nine	Working the Railway	49
Chapter Ten	Goods Traffic	57
Chapter Eleven	Accidents	59
Chapter Twelve	Locomotives (to 1923)	63
Chapter Thirteen	Carriages	85
Chapter Fourteen	Route and Stations	91
Chapter Fifteen	The Grouping and After	131
Chapter Sixteen	What Remains Today?	139
Appendix One	The Brecon Mountain Railway	141
Appendix Two	Working Timetable (Goods Trains) 1902	143
Appendix Three	Opening and Closing of Stations	156
	Authorities	157
	Index	159

D.S.M. Barrie, O.B.E.

Derek Barrie wrote authoritative articles and books over 60 years on a variety of railway subjects, but it was the railways of South Wales, where he spent his boyhood, that interested him most. His first book for the Oakwood Press, *The Taff Vale Railway*, was published in 1939. After distinguished War service, Derek Barrie returned to the Publicity Department of the LMS Railway, and after Nationalisation held many high administrative posts in British Railways; but he always found time for writing; his books for the Oakwood Press on the Rhymney, Brecon & Merthyr, and Barry Railways have, like the Taff Vale, been kept continuously in print over the years. He was at work on a new edition of the Brecon & Merthyr history when he became ill; he had collected all the new material but was not able to complete the actual writing. As his friend and publisher for 50 years I am glad to have been asked to complete the book for him, and I trust that what I have done will be considered up to the high standards he always set for himself.

R.W.K.

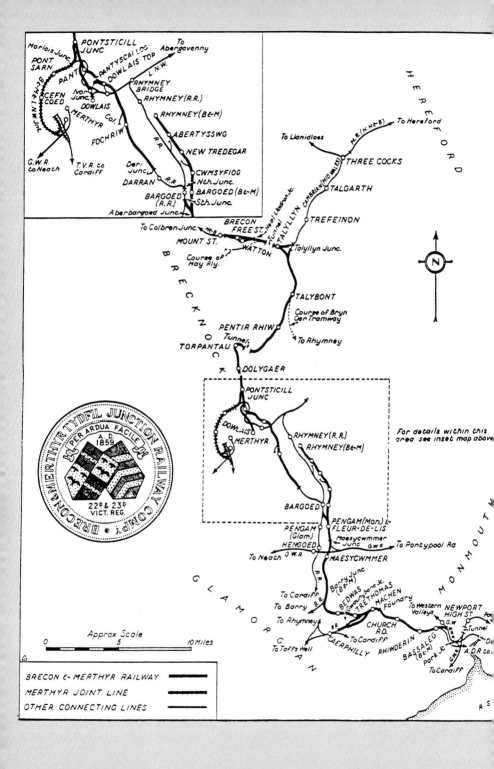

Introduction

It was in the last two years before World War I that as a small boy I first savoured the mysteries and excitements of railway enthusiasm, thanks to the proximity of house and school to the High Street station at Newport (Mon). This station accommodated passenger trains of three companies, and a frequent procession of goods trains of the owning company, the Great Western. The latter's superior stance was seen in its engines' gleaming brass chimney bands, rivalled only by the helmets of the Newport Fire Brigade. Moreover they displayed rolling history and geography lessons in the form of brass nameplates.

Neither of the two tenant companies could match this bravura, producing nothing better than small tank engines. The London & North Western coach livery was disliked by the younger set in reminding them of an unpopular school 'pud', rice and prunes. The third user, the Brecon & Merthyr, seemed a poor relation with its ill-assorted coaches of indeterminate livery. But to us and earlier generations of Newport folk this did not matter; it was a local and predominantly Welsh railway, going to places which we knew from childhood how to pronounce, such as Maesycymmer or Cwmsifiog. Affection was mingled with humorous contempt; the line was sometimes referred to as the 'Broke and Mortgaged'.

But why 'Brecon & Merthyr' we used to ask; why not Brecon & Newport? Brecon was 20 miles away from the most northern outcrop of the coalfield. True, it was a cathedral and garrison town at the confluence of two important rivers. But there were no collieries, no foundries, only sheep and forestry. In the 1850s when railways were expanding nationwide, the good men of Brecknockshire had their eyes on Newport and towns further south as outlets for their foodstuffs and timber, and long before the first train rolled into Brecon in 1863, rival promoters were seeing this line in the shadows of the Brecon Beacons as one link in a through railway route from the north to the South Wales ports. The complex and sometimes painful way in which that came about is described in this book. Sadly neither the Brecon & Merthyr nor the other two railways serving that city saw their centenary there, unless one counts the odd freight train which found its way to the Watton station for some two years after passenger services ceased in 1962. But that the line is by no means forgotten is proved by the call for this new edition of its history, 30 years after the first was published.

D.S.M.B.
June 1989

Pickering

PLACE NAMES: *for many Welsh place names there is no agreed spelling, and the spelling of some has varied over the years. In this book the names are given as generally used at the time referred to.*

Redwas station looking west about 1900. Note the signal box situated centrally on the platform to accommodate the view of the acute curve

Chapter One
A Railway of Character

The Brecon & Merthyr Railway ranked fifth in size among the score or so railways in the great industrial area of South Wales and Monmouthshire which operated independently of the invading English companies (Great Western, London & North Western, and Midland) until the railway 'grouping' of the 1920s. Hemmed in by rich and powerful neighbours like the Taff Vale and the Rhymney Railways, the Brecon & Merthyr was no doubt regarded as a poor relation with a distinctly murky past, which for half a century had struggled over mountains and against every kind of adversity to arrive at modest usefulness.

Nevertheless, on grounds of sheer interest, the Brecon & Merthyr was a very remarkable little railway. Embodying parts of two of the oldest tramroads in the country, it penetrated, by some of the most fearsome gradients and through some of the most superb scenery in the British Isles, a greater distance from the Bristol Channel into the hinterland of South Wales than any other local system save its neighbour and rival, the Neath & Brecon. Of its two tunnels, one was until closure the oldest in regular use, the other the highest above sea level, anywhere in Britain. Its history, too, matched these physical features in variety and interest: a history of staunch pioneering, of frenzied optimism and over-reaching ambition, and of a gallant, stubborn recovery from a period of receivership when even the rolling-stock was liable to seizure for debt; there are few more striking examples of the madcap railway economics of the mid-19th century. Even in a part of the country where almost all railways were on Chinese-laundry terms of mutual running powers and traffic agreements, the Brecon & Merthyr (B&M) was singularly prodigal both of its friendship and its enmity: it conceded running powers to eight different companies and enjoyed them over four, while there was one hectic period in the 1860s when each successive Parliamentary session found this vigorous, if virtually insolvent, little terrier of a railway launching out in several directions at once with proposals for new lines, junctions, running powers, and bids to lease or work neighbouring lines. It thought nothing of taking on as opponents half a dozen other railways at one time, including the Great Western and the London & North Western. It was one of the few smaller companies that had the temerity to reject acquisition by the Midland, and in all these circumstances its survival as an independent undertaking from 1859 until its absorption into the GWR under the Railways Act of 1921 was something of a miracle, akin to the continued co-existence of a lively little octopus in an aquarium full of sharks; periodically the octopus had some of its tentacles cut short, but none of the sharks was quite up to finishing it off.

Doubtful, perhaps, but never dull, the Brecon & Merthyr was a railway upon which it was always more amusing to travel than to arrive. And it was a railway full of 'characters' as well as character, for it was served with singular loyalty by a hard-worked staff, some of whom the company immortalised in its working time-tables, as mark the issue of 1902: 'Guard William Thomas [not just *the guard*] must see that hand-brake of van is properly screwed down before the Engine is cut off.' And how the readers of Railway

Clearing House circulars must have been uplifted by the magic-sounding place-names of Twynshon Evan Curve, Rising Sun Deviation, Seven Mile Bank, and Fleur-de-lis Machine Siding!

A headstone was erected in the chapel cemetery at Pentrupoel, Basseleg, inscribed 'by the workmen employed by the Brecon & Merthyr Railway as a tribute of respect for John Davies, Guard, who was accidentally killed on September 23rd 1870, age 31 years'. The stone carried a large and elaborate coat of arms, which was thought by many to be that of the railway, until somebody pointed out that it was in fact the Arms of the Oddfellows. The affection for the line persisted; at the time of the end of steam Fred Hando wrote movingly in the *South Wales Argus* of his recollections of the 'plucky 2−4−0 engine breathing hard and flushed brick red as he faced the stiff slope from Church Road to Machen'. It had been a different world; W.W. Tasker, whose father was often relief station man at Pont Sarn, told how this was a favourite place for a walk out from Merthyr in the evening; 'one evening 472 singles back to Merthyr were issued'.

Broadly speaking, the Brecon & Merthyr system comprised two separately constructed sections linked in the middle by running powers over 2¾ miles of the Rhymney Railway, and entered from the south by further powers over a similar mileage of Great Western tracks from Newport to Bassaleg. These two sections were the Southern, or 'Old Rumney', Section from Bassaleg to the ironworks town of Rhymney near the head of the Rhymney Valley, and the Northern or 'Brecon' Section from Deri Junction in the Bargoed Rhymney Valley through Pant, Pontsticill, and the mountains of the Brecon Beacons to Brecon.

The difference in character between the two halves of the system became marked at Pant; south of this point, the B&M was primarily a mineral line, industriously trundling long caravans of coal trucks down to Newport Docks; northwards, its character was like that of its rural neighbour, the Mid-Wales, with a sparse service of little passenger trains apt to drowse inconsequentially at remote junctions.

A journey from Brecon to Newport afforded a remarkable panorama of railways in Central and South Wales in pre-grouping days. In 47 miles the train passed through parts of three counties, Monmouth, Glamorgan and Brecknock; followed or crossed six major rivers; traversed 21 junctions, 12 of which were with 'foreign' railways, while the rolling stock of eight different companies would be seen *en route* (nine, if one made a diversion over the Merthyr branch from Pontsticill). Although the various routes will be described in detail later, it is necessary to set the scene at this point, so that the complex history which follows can be more easily understood.

Leaving the Great Western main line almost immediately west of Newport, B&M trains followed six tracks (four GWR, two Alexandra Docks & Railway) of the Tredegar Park 'Golden Mile' − so called because of the fortune in tolls paid out to the landowner − to their divergence at Bassaleg Junction; then across the River Ebbw on a fine masonry viaduct, turning into Bassaleg station, the location of the company's main locomotive depot, and freight yards. A short branch struck off north to serve some industrial plants, notably that of Nettlefolds (later GKN).

From Bassaleg the main B&M line now bore westwards into the Rhymney Valley on a sinuous upwards course to Machen, home of the B&M engine works and carriage repair depot and junction for the Caerphilly branch. At Trethomas and Bedwas, the first collieries made a strange contrast with the massive mediaeval bastions of Caerphilly Castle across the valley; here the Rhymney Railway came into view, and then the Barry Railway's spectacular viaduct straddling the valley to join the B&M as it turned north at Duffryn Isaf.

The Rhymney and B&M kept close company on their two sides of the valley, until after squeezing through a narrow arch of the viaduct carrying the former Newport, Abergavenny & Hereford Railway's Taff Vale Extension, the B&M divided at Aberbargoed Junction, 15 miles from Bassaleg; the Old Rumney Section went straight on for a further six miles up the east bank of the River Rhymney to its terminus at the town of that name, while the Brecon line dived through the reeking haze of the coke ovens and across the river into Glamorgan, to join the Rhymney Railway (RR) at Bargoed South Junction. Passing through Bargoed station, and leaving the main line of the RR immediately beyond it, B&M trains ascended the former's Bargoed Rhymney branch until passing again on to their own metals by an end-on junction at Deri.

Thus far the gradients, although rising continuously against the engine from Bassaleg, had not been arduous by the exacting standards of South Wales, but now as the Heads of the Valleys were approached there was a steady steepening to 1 in 40 for four miles past Deri Junction, the actual ruling grade being 1 in 38. At Pantywaen the labouring trains reached an altitude of 1,314 ft, when the railway began to cross a windswept tableland rejoicing in the name of Gelligaer Common. With the Bargoed Taff Joint Line of the Rhymney & Great Western almost in sight to the west on its way to Dowlais, the B&M also hastened thither across a desolation scarred by ancient ironstone pits and other industrial debris – a region dreaded for its winter snowdrifts. Now taking its own route through the once great 'iron-opolis' of Dowlais, with its four railway stations, some 350 ft higher than the town of Merthyr below, the line descended sharply from the plateau at Pant to be joined by the Merthyr branch at Pontsticill Junction, 27 miles and about 1 hour 40 minutes from Bassaleg.

Entering the old county of Brecknock and the valley of the Taf Fechan, with the towering bulwarks of the Brecon Beacons in full view to the north, the railway struck straight towards them by a three-mile ascent, mostly at 1 in 47 and 55, until reaching the second summit level, 1,313 ft at the west end of the Summit Tunnel, 666 yards long. Here in its wildest and most lonely situation, with scarcely a human habitation visible from Torpantau station, the line turned sharply eastwards through the tunnel, and then to the north again in the long descent through the magnificent scenery of Glyn Collwyn to the River Usk at Talybont (once rendered by London Parliamentary printers as 'Jalybout'!). This was the famous Seven Mile Bank, constructed throughout on a shelf cut into the hillside, and falling towards the River Usk for the first half-mile at 1 in 68 and then for 6½ miles at 1 in 38, so that southbound trains had to overcome a rise of 925 ft in seven miles.

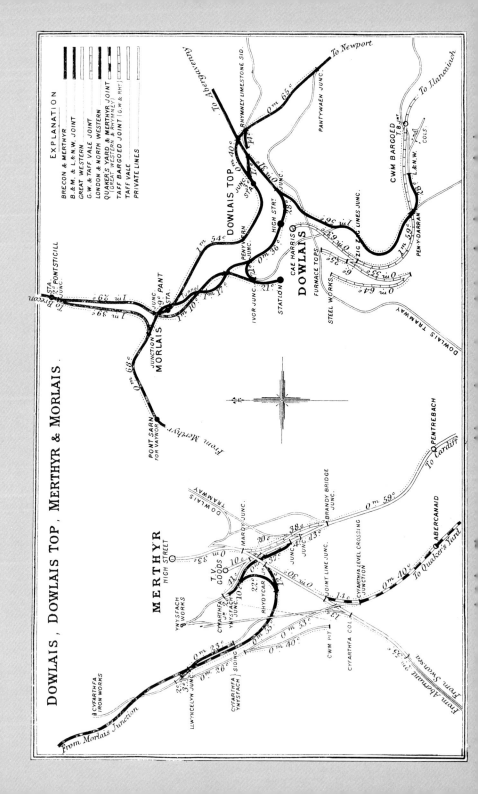

DOWLAIS, DOWLAIS TOP, MERTHYR & MORLAIS.

Near Talybont the railway crossed over the Brecknock & Abergavenny Canal and the River Usk, continuing northwards on the east side of both, until at Talyllyn Junction, with the Mid-Wales Railway coming in from the north, it turned west and through the tunnel and on to Brecon, a town served at one time and another by seven different railway companies.

Reference has been made above to the 'scarred landscape' of Merthyr and Dowlais. Although there was only a very small amount of ironmaking there in 1760, within 20 years the furnaces at Cyfarthfa, Plymouth, Penydarren and Dowlais were in full blast. By 1811 there were 150 miles of tramroads, and tentacles began to stretch to new pits, quarries and works. These had to be taken into account by the arriving 'real' railways. The B&M Act included safeguards for the Rhymney Limestone Railway, which ran from the Twynnau Gwynnion quarries across Dowlais Top to Rhymney, and other lines. Some had steam engines; these had begun in 1804 when Samuel Homfray bet Richard Crawshay that he could not carry 10 tons of iron at 5 mph from Thomas Town, Merthyr, down the Penydarren Plateway to Navigation at Abercynon. Trevithick provided the engine, which won the bet for Crawshay, but broke so many tramplates that the experiment was not followed up at the time! When imagining the scene, one must remember that Dowlais was high above Merthyr. The Dowlais Railway, which ran from the Taff Vale at Plymouth Ironworks to the Dowlais Works, began with a mile-long cable-worked incline (the reason why a passenger service over it was short-lived), and the tramways at the Merthyr level were also connected with those at the Dowlais level by two other quarter-mile inclines, the 'Bargoed Incline' and 'Penydarren Incline'.

A length of the combined edge-rail and tramplate track used by the 'Old Rumney' before it was taken over by the Brecon & Merthyr Railway.

Courtesy Railway Magazine

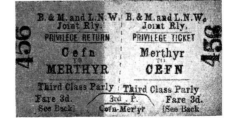

Chapter Two
The Beginning

Looking south in the 1850s a businessman in Brecon could see in his mind's eye the booming town of Merthyr, and Dowlais high on its hill above. But to go there, he was faced with a tortuous journey over indifferent toll roads. As early as 1838 a railway was proposed from Brecon to Merthyr via Talybont and the west sides of the Glyn and Taff Fechan Valleys. Sir John Guest of the Dowlais Ironworks was behind it, but no progress was made. The great ironmasters, Guest, Homfray, Crawshay, Wilkinson and Bacon were at the time satisfied with the Glamorganshire Canal, and with the tramroads joining the limestone quarries, coal pits and ironworks in a great lacing of mostly plateways, and with the Taff Vale Railway, connecting at the Plymouth Ironworks with the Dowlais Railway, which carried away their multifarious iron products. Guest at Dowlais, like his fellow Masters an immigrant from the Midlands, had rolled the first rails for the Liverpool & Manchester Railway. The canal was very profitable, making a revenue in 1853 of £150,000. Brecon too had its canal, the Brecknock & Abergavenny, but this turned east after Talybont and served only the eastern part of the industrial area.

Clearly a railway from Brecon to the south was needed and several local Brecon men set about planning it, chiefly the banker J.P. de Winton and solicitor John Cobb. Henry Conybeare, a local engineer, in 1856 surveyed a new route differing from the 1838 one in running down the east sides of the Glyn and Taff Fechan valleys. It was to terminate in the north at Talybont, because the Breconshire & Abergavenny Railway & Canal Company (B&A) had issued a prospectus for a railway along the route of the canal, and intended using some tramroad wayleaves to get to Crickhowell also. It was agreed between this company, and the Brecon & Merthyr Tydfil Railway Company, that the former would build the line from Talybont into Brecon, and the latter would receive running rights, though the terms for sharing receipts were the cause of some bickering.

Meanwhile the prospectus of the Brecon & Merthyr Tydfil Junction Railway had been issued, with a proposed capital of £150,000 in £10 shares. Hopes were expressed that 4½ miles of line at the Merthyr end would be worked jointly (presumably with the Merthyr, Tredegar & Abergavenny Railway (MT&A), later to be leased by the LNWR), and six miles of track at the Brecon end would be shared with the B&A, also the cost of the Usk bridge at Talybont. Pointing out that Brecon itself was excluded from the benefits of railway communication, although six railways had stations within 21 miles of the town, the prospectus painted a rosy picture not only of the opportunities which a railway would afford from marketing agricultural produce, but also of pleasure trips to the mineral springs of Central Wales and of day trips as far as Exeter by means of the Bristol Channel steamers and 'the Burnham branch of the Exeter Railway'. Moreover, 'a military force stationed at Brecon could . . . be rendered available for the protection of either of the important harbours on the northern coast of the Bristol Channel'. Receipts were estimated at £18,076 which, less expenses at 50 per cent, would return about 7 per cent on the proposed capital of

£130,000, although the fortunate shareholders 'might expect much more'. The joint Consulting Engineers, Conybeare and J.C. Birkinshaw, described the works as 'being of an easy character' and blandly dismissed the tremendous gradients of Seven Mile Bank in the sentence 'a good loco-motive road can be obtained throughout'.

The company's Bill, published on 8th November, 1858, named among the Directors J.P. de Winton (later elected Chairman), John Boyle, Chairman of the Rhymney Railway – which had opened its original main line that year, George Thomas Clark, one of the principals of the Dowlais Iron Company, and Henry Thomas, a Director of the Vale of Neath Railway. The railway was to extend from the New Racecourse at Brecon (near the head of the canal) along the south bank of the Usk to Talybont, and then over the route as eventually built to a junction with the Dowlais Railway, half a mile from the latter's Dowlais terminus.

The Brecon & Merthyr was to continue eastwards from Dowlais by two branches, each about 4½ miles long. One of these proposed branches was to connect with an authorised extension of the Rhymney Railway from the latter's main line at Bargoed to the Bargoed Rhymney Railway; the other was to go over the moors of Dowlais Top to the Rhymney Iron Works, thence to connect with the 'Old Rumney' Railway – the prefix, and Anglicised spell-ing of the last-named distinguishing it from its later and wholly Welsh namesake. The significance of the Old Rumney in the development of the Brecon & Merthyr becomes more evident at a later stage in this story.

During the progress of the B&M Bill, the branches towards the Rhymney Valley were dropped, apparently a temporary decison to counter possible objections from the Rhymney Iron Company, which feared the work might interfere with its operations.

There were, of course, many cross-currents in the tide of railway affairs. This is well illustrated by the prospectus of the Llanidloes & South Wales Railway Co., one of many which did not see the light of day. After reciting a route which was later that used by the Mid-Wales, down the Wye Valley, it stated that the line finished at Newbridge, as a new railway was in progress from the Shrewsbury & Hereford via Newbridge to Llandovery 'from whence a line is in course of construction to the existing Llanelly Railway'. Thus there were proponents of various lines coming from the east and others proposing lines from the north. Amongst the latter one of the most active was Benjamin Piercy, who acted as Engineer for many North Wales lines, and was in contact with John Cobb, of the Brecon law firm of Maybery Williams, & Cobb, which acted for the Brecon & Merthyr Railway.

The Mid-Wales Railway had originally intended to run from Newbridge to Llandovery, and applied to Parliament for powers; but at the same time the Central Wales Railway, a protégé of the London & North Western, applied for powers from Llandrindod Wells to Llandovery, which Parliament granted and threw out the Mid-Wales plan. Thus was the stage set for the latter to use Brecon for its southern terminus, a matter facilitated by the old Hay tramroad becoming available. In turn this meant that the great 'north to south' idea of Piercy and others would make use of the B&M line, and not any of the possible choices to the west. This is important, because although the company had so far only been considering how to get itself south, it soon became clear that much traffic would depend on there also being a satisfactory route from Brecon (or thereabouts) to the north.

A later possible competitor was the Sirhowy & Brecknock Junction Railway, which sought powers in 1861 to purchase the Bryn Oer Tramroad, but did not proceed. This tramroad ran from the canal wharf at Talybont over some very heavy country round a shoulder of rocks at Dyfryn Crawnon to the Trevil Quarries south of Mynydd Llangydnir, and then on to Bryn Oer Patch near Dowlais, where it connected with the Rhymney Ironworks tramways. They were not of the same gauge (the Rhymney one being wider) but a third set of plates was laid from there to the Ironworks so that stone wagons could enter. The Bryn Oer also brought timber for pit props from the Talybont area. In 1864 the Rhymney Ironworks, which had been carrying 180 tons of stone per week from Trevil Quarries on the line, gave it up because of rent rises forced by the Beaufort Estates. The north end was now rendered of little value by the arrival of the B&M, and the Bryn Oer ceased to run from 1865. For some reason in 1875 an Abandonment Act was thrown out by Parliament, but there is no evidence of working after 1865.

Before considering matters south of Merthyr, for the sake of clarity the history of the 'Brecon' portion of the B&M must be considered in more detail. In the town the Brecknock & Abergavenny Canal still exercised considerable influence. It was no local canal; by its junction with the Monmouthshire Canal south of Pontypool it gave access to Newport and many important industrial areas on the way. The Hay Tramroad running from its basin at Brecon (Watton) across the border to join the Kington tramroad meant that transport, cumbersome as it might be, was well established in a very wide area. Therefore when the canal company, as already mentioned, proposed to turn itself into a railway, it had the support of many people of influence, and when it appeared that the proposed Brecon & Merthyr Railway would be on the same course between Talybont and Brecon, the B&M agreed in December 1858 to delete that portion from its own Bill, and to negotiate terms for the use of the other company's rails.

However, the canal's railway, always referred to locally as the 'Breconshire', did not in fact secure as much finance as was expected, and its Parliamentary Bill was abruptly withdrawn, leaving no time for the Brecon & Merthyr to alter its own Bill before the First Reading in 1859. Thus when the Royal Assent was received on 1st August, 1859, the line appeared to start at Pant, which was not quite in Dowlais, and finish at Talybont, which was certainly not in Brecon. What was perhaps more serious, by this time two other companies had plans for Brecon: the Hereford, Hay & Brecon Railway (HH&B), and the Mid-Wales, which had been frustrated in its attempt to go to Llandovery and could really do no other than choose Brecon.

At just this time the ancient Hay Tramroad put itself up for sale; for 40 years its horse-drawn wagon trains had been part of the scenery, but life was changing. There followed some complex squabbling over possession of the body – not really a body as it was still working. There was strong opposition to the HH&B purchasing it, though much of the tramroad lay along its intended route. The HH&B was intending to run through the north part of

Brecon town and on to Swansea; but it really did not have the money. The B&M was anxious to restore its Talybont–Brecon link, and by using the tramroad, which had a tunnel to the east of Brecon which brought it into the town half-way up the hill, it would be better-placed than following the canal at the bottom of the valley. The Mid-Wales had a strong claim, since its intended route met the tramroad at Three Cocks (Glasbury) and its use would save it a very large mileage of construction.

In the end, everyone was happy; the HH&B got powers to take over the tramroad as far as Three Cocks, the Mid-Wales was given powers from there to what became Talyllyn Junction, and the B&M for the stretch into Watton. Accordingly in 1860 the companies obtained their Acts and gave each other mutual running powers. The B&M Act allowed the abandonment of its original route along the south bank of the Usk into Brecon, in favour of a 2½ mile line along the east bank from Talybont to the Tallyllyn Tunnel, or rather a point three chains short of this, where the Mid-Wales Railway joined, and both were to send their trains through the tunnel; the HH&B in its turn got powers to run over the Mid-Wales and B&M from Glasbury into Brecon (Watton). The B&M's portion of the old Hay was four miles long, but it included the 674 yds-long tramroad tunnel, which needed widening and deepening to take full-gauge rail traffic; for this an increase of capital of £50,000 was asked for and granted.

The 1860 Acts did not in fact prove to be very effective instruments. The tramroad obstinately continued to run its trains, even though the trackbed was sold, raising various points of Parliamentary and legal procedure, so that in 1861 the B&M and Mid-Wales companies had to go back to Parliament for a further Act forcing the tramroad to allow their Engineers unrestricted access to the sites. It is easy to see that users of the tramroad would wish to continue; it would be four years before someone in Hay could send his goods by rail to Brecon; what were they to do in the meantime? One problem however was disposed of at this time; the HH&B, which had been loudly claiming that it would construct its own route to Merthyr, announced that this had been dropped.

Construction began as was customary with the cutting of the first sod; however in this case there were two ceremonies, one each side of the site of Torpantau Tunnel on 18th January, 1860. On the Merthyr side the act was done by the Reverend John Williams of Coity Mawr, and on the Brecon side by Howell Richards, the joint owner of the land. The weather was terrible, but 50 persons turned up, briefly. The well-known David Davies of Llandinam filled the first barrow, stating with typical media sense that 'a contractor ought to know well the work that he would summon other men to do'. The *Merthyr Star* which duly picked this remark up, referred to him as contractor also, though his appointment was not ratified until August. On 17th July a letter signed 'Davies, Savin & Ward' was sent to the B&M Board offering to construct the line, supply locomotives and rolling stock, and to work the line for 10 years, for a mixture of cash and shares. The partners guaranteed the shareholders a payment of 5 per cent of total cost for the period during which they worked the line, a very favourable offer. This method had been employed by Davies & Savin with a number of Welsh

ANNO VICESIMO SEPTIMO & VICESIMO OCTAVO

VICTORIÆ REGINÆ.

****

Cap. cclxv.

An Act to authorize certain Deviations from the existing and authorized Lines of the *Brecon and Merthyr Tydfil Junction* Railway Company, and to empower that Company to form a Junction with the Limestone Railway of the *Rhymney* Iron Company, and (instead of the *Vale of Neath* Railway Company) to exercise the Powers of the *Vale of Neath* Railway Act, 1863, for constructing the *Merthyr* Curve; and to raise further Monies; and for other Purposes.

[25th *July* 1864.]

WHEREAS by "The *Brecon and Merthyr Junction* Railway Act, 1859," (herein-after called "the original Act,") the *Brecon and Merthyr Tydfil Junction* Railway Company (herein-after called the "*Brecon* Company") were incorporated: And whereas the following Acts relating to the *Brecon* Company have since been passed: (namely,) "The *Brecon and Merthyr*

22 & 23 Vict. c. lxviii.

23 & 24 Vict. c. xviii.

[*Local.*]

The title page of one of three Acts applied for in 1864. The Rhymney Limestone Railway ran from Twynnau Gwynnion quarries north of Dowlais across the route of the B&M at Pantywaun and on to the Rhymney Ironworks. The deviations were the 'Dowlais Road Side Pond' and others at Machen and Bedwas.

railways; they had been appointed by the Mid-Wales, but some of the Directors did not like their style, and they withdrew from the contract before work started.

Davies was a brilliant engineer and promoter, later a wealthy man and owner of the Ocean Collieries. Thomas Savin was different; energetic, ambitious, and self-taught in engineering and railway matters. His partnership with Davies was recent and was not to last; when they became involved a year later with the Aberystwyth & Welsh Coast Railway, they differed on a matter of policy, believed to be Savin's desire to build a number of hotels, and they parted. However Savin with his brother-in-law Ward continued with the B&M and several other contracts. The Engineers appointed for the B&M were Birkinshaw & Conybeare of London. However the detailed work was done by Alexander Sutherland, working for the contractors. It was he who supervised the difficult work of piercing the Torpantau Tunnel. This was cut through on 11th January, 1862 and made suitable for traffic in August. It was 663 ft long, slightly shorter than the tunnel at Talyllyn. The latter ranked until closure as the oldest railway tunnel still in use – that is if one considers the airspace rather than the walls and floor, which were new.

The approach of the railway from the south was keenly awaited by the public in Brecon and around. Although in England and South Wales most people had by now seen a railway train, this was not the case in Mid-Wales. The contractors, Savin & Ward, had purchased one of the first 0–6–0ST engines of the famous makers Manning, Wardle & Co., named *Pioneer*, and this reached Dowlais in December 1861; it was shortly joined by another named *Usk*. These became familiar sights south of Torpantau Tunnel, and after the tunnel bore was completed a special train for Directors and friends was run from Pen-north (4½ miles from Brecon) to Pant on 28th August, 1862. It was hauled by *Pioneer*, and another engine, *de Winton*, was added at Torpantau. On New Year's Day 1863 a ballast train actually reached Brecon, again with *Pioneer*. On 20th January there was a major trial run: *Usk* left Brecon with several carriages, picked up *Pioneer* and more carriages at Talyllyn, and at the tunnel was joined by *de Winton* and more carriages; the whole triple-headed assembly then proceeded to Pant. On the return trip, the train seems to have been split, one portion bringing to Brecon the first load of coal from the south. At a Board Meeting in February, 1863 the Chairman reported that goods traffic was already in operation between Pant and Brecon.

The first official passenger train ran on 23rd April, 1863 from Brecon; however from 19th March two trains per day had been running between Talybont and Pant with coach connections to Merthyr and Brecon; a third (early morning) service was added in May. There were stations at Talyllyn (or Brynderwen), Talybont, which had a solid little engine shed and turntable, Dolygaer and Pant. At his inspection of the line in February, Capt. J.H. Rich for the Board of Trade had complained that Pant station was on a 1 in 47 gradient, but accepted that this was only a temporary station. He had other worries; there was a catch siding at Talybont at the end of the seven-mile bank, but he felt it would be better to increase braking power and make sure there was nothing to catch. He passed the line from Pant to Talybont at a later inspection, on 16th March, and the remainder on 22nd April.

Somewhat unusually, the great celebration train trip and banquet were held after the service began, on 1st May, 1863. Two 0–6–0 tender engines, *Vulcan* and *de Winton* were chosen to haul the special train; bands played at Brecon both for the departure and return, and also at Pant. The local press was ecstatic; tribute was paid to H. Conybeare, the Chief Engineer; an official from the Taff Vale Railway was present, but apparently no one from the Mid-Wales or HH&B; perhaps the fact that they were still struggling to get their lines open made the occasion too painful.

There was no station at Torpantau, but there was a siding and probably a loop; it is known that passengers sometimes used it, but no platform was erected for some years. Likewise Pentir Rhiw was not an original station but a passing loop and signal box; it became a conditional stop only in 1909.

Talybont was equipped with a 1,200 gallon water tank, placed beside the station building on the up platform; about a mile of conduit pipe was needed to fill this from mountain streams. People have expressed surprise that a station was built at Dolygaer in such remote countryside. However, the Merthyr Tydfil Board of Health had created a reservoir at nearby Pentwyn, about a mile long and half a mile wide, and at the time the B&M was opening it was announced that steam pleasure boats would be put on this lake. One at least did operate from about 1866, as well as other smaller boats, and it became a favourite resort for week-end enjoyment; especially so after the branch to Cefn was opened, and long excursion trains brought in the workers from the Merthyr area, and in particular the Cyfarthfa Ironworks. During the summer regatta at Pentwyn trains ran every half-hour from Cefn to Dolygaer.

In Brecon, the terminus was at Watton, near the canal basin. This was only a single platform and it seems that even then it was the intention to build a permanent station at a higher level, though much discussion was to take place over this. At Watton, there was an engine shed and turntable for the use of the 'Savin' railways, the Brecon & Merthyr and Hereford Hay & Brecon; a shed would also be put up by the Mid-Wales Railway. There were goods sidings also, though much of the goods was to run via the east loop at Talyllyn and the goods sidings there were more extensive. The ownership of the lines at Talyllyn was: north and east loops, half each B&M and Mid-Wales, south loop B&M only. However various uses were made of the space within the triangle (later the B&M built an engine shed which could only be reached over Mid-Wales metals), and when Capt. Mark Huish of the LNWR (retired) was asked to arbitrate over various matters of dispute between the B&M and the Mid-Wales at their jointly-used stations, he was unable to sort out matters at Talyllyn, merely recommending that things stay as they were.

For over a year the B&M did not connect with anything at Talyllyn, and the temporary station at Brynderwen, at the west junction of what would later be a triangle, served only a few cottages. The Mid-Wales Railway started by completing the north curve, giving access to Brecon. However it seems that to Savin, and possibly the B&M Board, this was not the most

TO
Alfred Henshaw Esquire.

Dear Sir,

The Officers and Staff of the **Brecon** and **Merthyr Railway Company** feel that they cannot permit the occasion of your severing your connection with the Company, extending over the long period of thirty one years, without offering for your acceptance this ADDRESS and accompanying PORTRAIT, and at the same time desire to express their regret at your resigning the position you have held so long and honorably, and the duties of which you have discharged with such efficiency and so much credit to yourself, and also in losing the benefit of a supervision exercised with so much kindness and consideration.

We desire to assure you of our best and heartiest wishes for your future happiness and prosperity both in your business and domestic relations.

I am, Dear Sir,

On behalf of the Committee and Subscribers,

Yours faithfully,

NEWPORT
JULY
1894

The illuminated address given to Alfred Henshaw on his retirement from the General Managership of the railway in 1894, a position he had occupied since 1863.

D.S. Barrie Collection

The ornate 'monogram' coat of arms of the Brecon & Merthyr Railway.
D.S. Barrie Collection

The portrait of Alfred Henshaw, General Manager from 1863 to 1894, referred to in the illustrated address on the opposite page. *D.S. Barrie Collection*

important side. At a Board Meeting in 1863, after the train service to Pant had started, Savin made a comment that 'your railway ends in a ploughed field, but the Mid-Wales Railway will shortly honour its undertaking', which suggests that in his mind the East Loop, allowing through running from the Mid-Wales line to Pant, ought to take priority. In fact this was the last bit of construction and probably did not open until 19th September, 1864, at the same time that Mid-Wales and HH&B passengers services into Brecon began. Both Benjamin Piercy, who was heavily involved in the Mid-Wales and the lines which would shortly be gathered together as the Cambrian Railways, and Savin, had planned for years to build a north to south trunk route. Savin was already, in effect, running railways from Oswestry to Llanidloes; John Cobb had been recruited by Piercy to offer the B&M as part of the route, and the Mid-Wales was not averse to it, so the tardiness over the East Loop at Talyllyn was naturally galling. However, it must be said that the B&M was also having trouble in providing a more important link in the north–south chain at Dowlais. There were also worries closer to Brecon.

In 1863 the Dulais Valley Mineral Railway, which had been incorporated in the previous year to connect Neath with some collieries between there and Ollwyn, decided to apply for an Act to change its name to the Neath & Brecon Railway (N&B), to extend its railway to that town, and to make arrangements with the HH&B and with the B&M. The provision regarding the former was alarming to the latter; the HH&B plan to take its railway through Bronllys and north of Brecon to connect with the N&B would take traffic away and threaten Conybeare's idea of a joint station. Moreover, the N&B sought powers to build across country from Devynock to connect with the Central Wales line at Llangamarch or Llandovery, so opening up a route from the Midlands to Swansea and West Wales. The N&B obtained the powers in 1864, although the B&M had its own Brecon & Llandovery scheme in hand, authorised a year before. The B&M now led its ace of trumps, a Bill introduced for the 1864 Session to authorise the sale or lease to it of both the HH&B and its protégé the Kington & Eardisley Railway, for which purpose it sought to raise a further £600,000 by preference shares and mortgages.

The Bill emerged with the reference to the Kington & Eardisley deleted, under the title Brecon & Merthyr (Amalgamation) Act, of 5th July, 1865, and took effect three weeks later. With its eastern flank now secure, the B&M could afford to offer an end-on junction with the N&B 19 chains west of its intended joint station. There is usually some one person who acts as a catalyst in these complex arrangements, and in this case it seems to have been William Laurence Banks, of Watton House, who from being Company Secretary of the HH&B, emerged now as Chairman of the B&M (succeeding J.P. de Winton, though two other members of the family joined the Board), and was at the same time Chairman of the N&B and a Director of the Brecon & Llandovery Junction Railway! However, it seems to have been a case of 'more haste, less speed', because a few years later it was found that as the shareholders had not been consulted about the take-over of the HH&B, it was invalid, and in 1868 a further Act forced a 'disamalgamation' and the temporary reconstitution of the HH&B.

Meanwhile at the beginning of 1866, Thomas Savin, who with John Ward had been managing the railway (and paying the shareholders their guaranteed 5 per cent), was overwhelmed by his commitments and failed disastrously, nearly bringing down the Brecon & Merthyr with him. The crisis found the company not merely without a dividend for the second half of 1865, but having over-expended its capital account, being heavily in debt to sundry creditors, and with its Merthyr branch unfinished; moreover, until it was finished, the through route to Newport could not be brought into use. In 1866 the company failed to pay interest on any of its debentures; litigation by creditors and the appointment of a receiver by the Chancery Court followed. It took the next two years to obtain some sort of order in the company's affairs, this being achieved by the B&M Arrangement Act of July 13th, 1868 and by a scheme of arrangement with the creditors confirmed by the court on 22nd January, 1870. These provided for the conversion of the mortgage and debenture debts into debenture stock; revision of the capital and raising of fresh capital; suspension of all legal proceedings against the company for 10 years, except by leave of the court; and reconstitution of the Directorate to include representatives of the mortgagees. The rolling stock, which had been liable to seizure by creditors and much of which had been sold subject to power of redemption, became vested in the Directors on trust for the mortgagees and other creditors. Receivership combined with the legal separation from the HH&B gave the Board many headaches. It had already become disenchanted with running the Hereford trains, and persuaded the Mid-Wales Railway to take this on as from 1st October, 1868. A year later the Midland Railway took over, and the B&M had rid itself of its Hereford commitment.

An event of 1865 which was of little effect on the B&M was the sale of the Brecon & Abergavenny Canal to the Monmouthshire Railway (for £70,000 less than it cost to build). The politics of this lie outside the area of present concern, but it did later give the Great Western Railway an early stake in Brecon, for it absorbed the Monmouthshire Railway long before the lines at Brecon fell into its hands in 1922.

Almost from the start the B&M had trouble with its six-span wooden bridge over the Usk at Talybont, which began visibly to sag. In 1869 it was decided to build a stronger structure alongside and slew the track when it was completed. It was also decided to build this for double track. Owing to frequent 'wild-runs' down the seven-mile-bank, to be described later, the passing loop at Talybont had been progressively lengthened, and now extended over the Usk bridge and 300 yards into the Llansantffraid cutting, thus giving a better chance for northbound trains to get under control without endangering approaching southbound trains.

Brecon Free Street Station viewed from the east on 11th September, 1951 with No. 52525 on the local Hereford service just about to depart from the bay platform.

H.C. Casserley

A fine early 1920 view of Brecon Free Street station viewed this time from the west showing the large decorative station buildings. *Lens of Sutton*

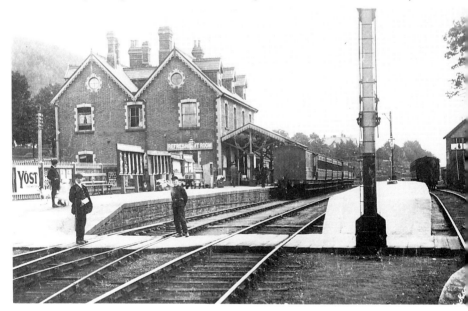

Chapter Three
Completion to Merthyr

When Capt. Rich carried out his second inspection of the line on 16th March, 1863 he had stated '. . . the portion of the line on which the temporary station at Pant is situated . . . now becomes only a branch line to the main line, which turns off to Tredegar at 18¾ miles'. It seems therefore that the first Pant station was on the Dowlais line, while the second was at the junction with the main line, running south to join with the Rhymney Railway. The management certainly had not lost sight of their main objective: to become a through route from Central Wales down into the smoke-hung amphitheatre of Merthyr, where the great ironmasters were piling up slag heaps and fortunes, but also through the rich valleys beyond, with their fast-developing coal measures, to the Bristol Channel ports. No doubt these thoughts were encouraged by the reflection that 19 miles of railway through mountains largely populated by sheep were not likely to sustain a guaranteed 5 per cent dividend.

It is indeed remarkable that during this period of tribulation the railway was completed. The key to the situation was the Merthyr branch; the saviour of the venture was Alexander Sutherland, C.E., who had supervised the bridges at Talybont, and who produced an alternative route into Merthyr which avoided Cyfarthfa Castle by going down the west side, and so won the support instead of the enmity of the Crawshay family. This success was achieved at great engineering expense, however, the 6¾ miles between Pontsticill and Merthyr involving an almost continuous descent at 1 in 45–50 and (between Morlais Junction and Merthyr) two complete reversals of direction; the home signal governing the admission of a B&M train to Merthyr station was first seen from its back! Moreover, two great stone-arch viaducts were required to carry the line over the Taf Fechan and the Taf Fawr (the main river) at Pontsarn and Cefn Coed respectively. The former was 455 ft long and 92 ft high, comprising seven arches of 40 ft 6 in. span and a massive abutment, originally planned as an eighth arch, at the Merthyr end. Cefn Coed or Pontycapel viaduct was 770 ft long and 115 ft high, consisting of 15 arches of 39 ft 6 in. span.

After Savin's failure, the B&M Directors asked Sutherland to complete the Merthyr branch, on which work had temporarily come to a stop, with Pontycapel viaduct unfinished. (At about this time, Henry Conybeare became Consulting Engineer to the B&M, instead of Engineer.) Mrs Sutherland ceremonially laid the last brick in September 1866, but there was a further interruption due to contracting difficulties, and it was not until 1st August, 1867 that the line was opened from Pontsticill to Cefn, which then replaced Pant as the terminal for the Merthyr horse-bus.

The Brecon & Merthyr's terminal arrangements in Merthyr itself were not completed without difficulties with both the Taff Vale (TVR) and the mixed-gauge Vale of Neath Railway (V of N); a B&M intervention in the Bill (1865) for the amalgamation of the V of N with the GWR led to the Bill having to be hastily withdrawn when the Commons committee showed itself ready to grant the B&M running powers via the Vale of Neath into Swansea! The Bill went through, without this contentious provision, in the following year, and it was agreed that the B&M should join the Vale of Neath at Rhydycar Junction, ½-mile south-west of the latter's High Street passenger station, which was to be used by B&M trains. (The Taff Vale also transferred its passenger services to it in 1878.) Two short branches were also made off the B&M line between Cefn and Rhydycar Junction, one from Llwyncelyn Junction to connect with the Cyfarthfa Iron Works private lines and another to give access to the TVR goods lines and to Ynysfach Iron Works.

Completion of the Merthyr branch for public services on 1st August, 1868 left the Brecon & Merthyr legally free to complete its through route from Brecon to Newport. This had been publicly opened over the 1¾ miles from Pant to Dowlais Top on 1st August, 1867, and at long last the line was officially brought into use between Dowlais Top and Pengam on 1st September, 1868, with a weekday service of three trains each way daily between Brecon and Newport (Dock Street). This service was diverted to the High Street station in Newport on the opening of the Great Western loop line between Park and Gaer Junctions on 11th March, 1880.

In order to improve its access to the town and works of Dowlais after the abandonment of a planned junction with the Dowlais Railway, the Brecon & Merthyr obtained powers in 1865 for a single-line branch 1¼ miles long from Pant to a high-level terminus at Lloyd Street, Dowlais, adjoining the Ivor Works. This branch was opened on 23rd June, 1869; it fell most of the way from Pant, with a ruling descent of 1 in 40, and a curious feature at the Dowlais end was that there were two signal boxes, Dowlais No. 1 and Dowlais No. 2 Junctions (the former being known in B&M days as Ivor Junction), which were only 12 ch. apart, while a third (ex-LNWR) box at Penywern Junction was only ¼ mile distant. The only intermediate station (later a halt) on the branch, Pantyscallog, was opened in June 1911.

In his Report of the year to 31st December, 1870, the Chairman was optimistic. The 'disamalgamation' of the HH&B had been completed, costing the B&M £7,000, but as regards the Savin mess, the Company had been unable to obtain any satisfaction. The B&M now had 25 engines, 13 tenders, 33 carriages and four passenger guards vans. The best news however was that the new Brecon station at Free Street would be open by 18th March, 1871 and thus 'the line between Heol Lladron and Heolrhydd, hitherto unproductive, will be utilised. A main line is thus completed between Hereford, Neath and Swansea'. Understanding of this statement requires a hard look at the complex matter of the Brecon stations.

Chapter Four
Brecon Joint Station

The station arrangements at Brecon must have been confusing for passengers in the early years, and have not been entirely disentangled by historians, because timetables only quoted 'Brecon' without detailing which station was concerned. When the three companies first arrived, a station was erected by the B&M just above the canal basin, Watton station. This included an engine shed, turntable, and goods sidings, and at the west end a single rather rough platform with a low building. This was on the north side of the track, which went on, how early cannot be stated for sure, up a gradient to join a higher level track, which was laid about 1866 from Heol Lladron, later called Brecon Junction, 25 chains east of Watton, to Heolrhydd where the Free Street bridge was shortly to be built by the Neath & Brecon Railway.

The Neath & Brecon Railway was not welcomed in Brecon by the B&M, but had made an agreement to meet end-on at the east side of Free Street, this point being 55 chains from Heol Lladron. A temporary station called Mount Street was put up by the Neath & Brecon 12 chains further west from the junction. Meanwhile conditions at Watton became somewhat congested, and the Mid-Wales, in spite of having erected its own engine shed there beside the 'Savin' one, elected to use Mount Street as its passenger terminus from 1868.

There was a general agreement that a single station for joint use was required. There were several problems; the Board of Trade was not happy about the bridge over Free Street, and forbade trains from Neath from using it. At a Parliamentary enquiry in 1869, an official from the N&B stated that if passengers from Neath for stations further east arrived at Mount Street, they were put on an engine and taken to a point on the high level line above Watton, where they were dropped. The reason for this was that the B&M, who controlled the lower line down to Watton, would not allow N&B trains to use it. This is at odds with the fact that Mid-Wales Railway trains were using Mount Street, crossing the Free Street Bridge.

After a good deal of lobbying as to whether the 'joint' station should be at Mount Street or Free Street, the latter was chosen, and the B&M put in hand the building of a handsome station, at the point where the line up from Watton joined the high level line. The contract was for £2,000, but this was no doubt somewhat overspent. The station buildings included offices for all the companies using it; the Mid-Wales was allowed to have a permanent official there. The main (north) platform had a short bay facing Talyllyn; on the south side there was an island platform; a signal box was located beside the south loop, and from here the line, referred to locally as 'the straight siding' ran down to Watton. Engines needed to use this to reach or leave the shed, but for turning, a table was later added on a spur from the east end of the main platform.

Free Street station was opened for traffic on 1st March, 1871; on 1st May the Mid-Wales, which had reverted to Watton, began to use it, and the Neath & Brecon service also started and terminated there, Mount Street being closed except for goods traffic. It has been mentioned that the Midland Railway took over the working of the trains from Hereford on 1st October,

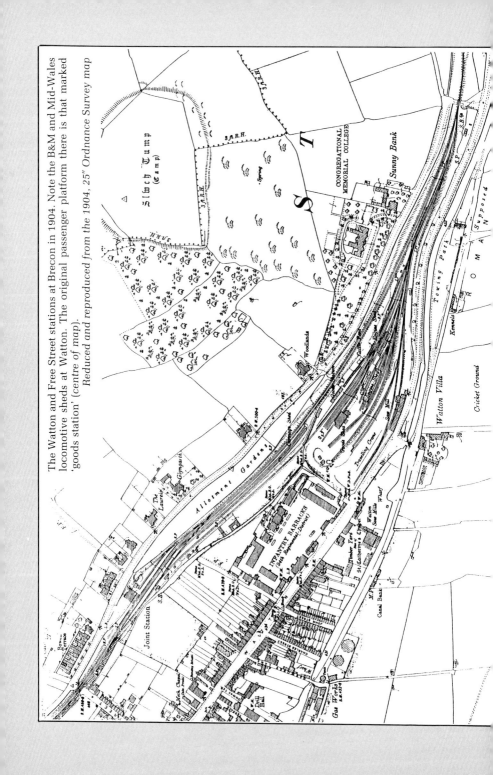

The Watton and Free Street stations at Brecon in 1904. Note the B&M and Mid-Wales locomotive sheds at Watton. The original passenger platform there is that marked 'goods station' (centre of map).
Reduced and reproduced from the 1904, 25" Ordnance Survey map

The original Brecon terminus at Watton seen from the west; the line continues on the left up to the Brecon Free Street station. *Author's Collection*

The Watton station platform and station buildings viewed from the east. *Author's Collection*

1869, and these trains used Watton terminus and Free Street when opened.

There have been confusing statements about the date at which the Neath & Brecon trains began to use Free Street, but an extant letter to the N&BR Directors stating 'This company's trains have this morning commenced running into the new station', dated 6th March, 1872, seems to settle the matter. However, the reason why the Board of Trade permitted Mid-Wales Railway trains to use Mount Street on 22nd October, 1868, but refused to allow N&B trains to use the connection to the B&M on 8th February, 1871 is not clear, apart from a suggestion that improvement of signalling at the N&BR/B&M junction was required – a junction which was already being run over by the Mid-Wales.

It was also decided to have a joint station at Talyllyn; that is, jointly used – it belonged to the B&M. It was built at the West Junction, approximately in the same place as the temporary Brynderwen station, right up against the mouth of the tunnel; visibility was so restricted by the tunnel that special warning lights were set up inside it. It was opened on 1st October, 1869; while it had been building, B&M trains used the Mid-Wales station at the North Junction, shunting up the East Loop to reach it. The Mid-Wales station had platforms on both the North and East Loops, the latter for the benefit of through trains from north to south. The two stations were some 400 yds apart, and it seems probable that B&M trains had always called at their own Brynderwen station and at the Mid-Wales one for interchange of passengers, for a Board Minute of August 1869 refers to 'alterations at the Brynderwen station so as to render it unnecessary for trains to run up to Talyllyn station proper'.

The Mid-Wales station was not closed until 1878, though it was probably only used by through trains after 1869, at which time the Mid-Wales trains to Brecon used the new joint station. Thereafter through trains were shown in the tables as stopping at Talyllyn, but in fact they remained in the East Loop while engines were changed.

Meanwhile the Midland Railway had been setting up various deals whereby it could reach Swansea using the metals of the Neath & Brecon Railway from Brecon as far as Ynysygeinon Junction. It offered to lease this line, if it was put into good running order; however the N&B had no money to do this, and the Midland had to refurbish it itself. From 2nd July, 1877 the trains from Hereford were extended through Brecon to Swansea, and also carried through carriages from Birmingham. The N&B withdrew its own trains from Brecon as at that date.

Also in 1877 a fire occurred at Free Street station. An article in *The Locomotive* in 1921 stated that it was burnt down and a new one built, but there is no evidence for this. Other writers have stated that it was Watton that was burnt down. However, a letter from the General Manager's 'temporary office at Watton' dated 1877 makes it clear that the fire was at Free Street, and serious enough to make the office uninhabitable, but probably doing no great damage to the structure.

Chapter Five
Looking Southwards

It is now necessary to go back 10 years or more to the problems faced by the B&M promoters in gaining entry to South Wales proper. South of Merthyr and Rhymney, the Taff Vale Railway – oldest, strongest, and wealthiest of the South Wales Railways – was firmly in possession of the route from Merthyr down to Cardiff, while the Rhymney Railway was established astride the Rhymney Valley route to the port. In 1854 these two companies had been allies, but friction had developed between them, and in the year of the Brecon & Merthyr's incorporation they were engaged in furious warfare. Each was therefore equally suspicious of any overtures by the B&M towards the other; as the B&M sought the favours of both while at the same time indicating plainly its intentions to win through to the sea, the little company drew down upon itself the embattled wrath of two powerful antagonists, neither of whom was on speaking terms with the other until it came to fighting a common foe.

Thus, while its main line was still under construction, the B&M solicited Taff Vale support for a direct connection at Merthyr itself, in place of the awkward link via the Dowlais Railway embodied in its Act. In treating these overtures with coolness, and ignoring a provision made by the B&M in its Extensions Act of 1860 for the Taff Vale to subscribe up to £30,000, the latter was probably influenced by the recollection that Conybeare's surveyors, when attempting to plot a route down through Taf Fechan in 1857, had been incontinently ejected by William Crawshay, the Cyfarthfa ironmaster, from his Cyfarthfa Castle grounds. No doubt the Taff considered it tactful towards an important customer to profess the gradients of such a route to be impracticable.

In the following year, 1861, however, when the Brecon & Merthyr went to Parliament with a revival of its proposal for a branch down the Bargoed Rhymney Valley, the TVR, loudly protesting at the non-completion of the Dowlais Railway connection, managed to secure the insertion by the Commons committee of a clause that no part of this Bargoed branch was to be opened for traffic until the B&M should have completed its authorised junction with the Dowlais Railway 'or in lieu thereof any line which might be authorised by Parliament to connect the B&M with the TVR at Merthyr'. (In all subsequent relevant legislation the B&M was unable to secure any significant modification of the restriction, the effect of which was considerably to delay the opening of its line to Bargoed.)

The importance of the Dowlais Ironworks in the area can be guessed from the fact that in the 1840s 12,000 men were employed there. It had been first set up in 1760; by 1900 it was the last iron and steel works in Glamorgan, but it did not finally close down until 1987. There had been a canal from Merthyr to the ironworks, replaced by a railway, the Dowlais Railway, in 1851. In due course the Dowlais Railway was connected at Merthyr with the LNWR, TVR and B&M, and at Dowlais with the Rhymney Railway; it ceased working in 1930.

Reaction of the Rhymney Railway to the Bargoed branch revival was even more vigorous, and the differences which arose on this issue (stimulated by

A northbound train headed by 0–6–0ST No. 18 (ex No. 11) leaving Merthyr *c*1920.
L.C.G.B., Ken Nunn Collection

The same train is seen here between Merthyr and Cefn. *L.C.G.B., Ken Nunn Collection*

suspicion of the Brecon & Merthyr's territorial ambitions and of its recent approach to the Taff Vale) led to the resignation of John Boyle, the Rhymney Chairman, from the B&M Board and to many years' bitter rivalry between the two companies. The immediate row over the Bargoed Rhymney branch was due to the B&M seeking, in its Bill for 1861, not merely to join up with the RR branch through the valley (for which the Rhymney had obtained powers in 1854 but never exercised them) but to go right down to Bargoed and join the Rhymney there. Now at Groesfaen, at the lower end of the valley, the ravine would admit of no more than one railway, and the only practicable route was occupied by the surveyor's pegs of both companies. Seeking no doubt to afford fair play to both, Parliament passed both the B&M branch and the Rhymney's revival of its earlier scheme, but inserted, in the B&M (Extensions) Act of 6th August, 1861, no less than 2½ pages of mutually restrictive clauses. This Gilbertian situation produced a stalemate in the Bargoed Rhymney Valley lasting two years, to be succeeded by the almost inevitable compromise.

As the Second Railway Mania neared its climax, the Brecon & Merthyr forged ahead – on paper. In 1862 it obtained powers to abandon the unwanted connection with the Dowlais Railway and to make instead a line to the Taff Vale at Merthyr, the TVR being offered (though it did not accept) the opportunity to subscribe a further £30,000. The same Act authorised an eastward extension of the B&M through Dowlais Top to join, near Nantybwch, the Sirhowy Railway's connection to the Merthyr, Tredegar & Abergavenny Railway. This eastward extension, which never came to fruition, represented an abortive attempt on the part of the B&M to hold back the advance towards Merthyr of the London & North Western Railway.

The Brecon & Merthyr's next, and more profitable, move was to acquire the so called 'Old Rumney'. This had been incorporated, as a tramroad, as early as 20th May, 1825 and opened with horse traction in the following year. It began at Pwll-y-Llaca, Abertysswg, south of Rhymney and ran down the east side of the Rhymney Valley, being later paralleled on the west side, near to Caerphilly, by the Rhymney Railway. Above Caerphilly the Old Rumney bore eastward through Machen to Bassaleg, and its significance lay in its connection at Pye Corner below Bassaleg with the Nine Mile Point Tramroad (Monmouthshire Canal Co.), which was an extension of the Sirhowy Railway and ran into Newport, and over which the Rumney had running powers. A private tramway from Pwll-y-Llaca to the Rhymney Ironworks was also sanctioned.

Long before the Brecon & Merthyr and the Rhymney Railways came into the picture, the Old Rumney had become notorious for the condition of its track (combined flange- and edge-rails) and for the congestion upon it of horse-drawn coal trams, gigs, carts, and pedestrians. Since 1854 at latest, steam locomotives had been added to these perils, subject to a 10 mph speed restriction. With a view to modernising the line, the undertaking was reincorporated as the Rumney Railway Company by Act of 1st August, 1861, which authorised an expansion of capital for purposes of improvement, including adaptation for passenger traffic, and the construction of a branch from Machen to the Rhymney Railway near Caerphilly. Powers were also

Merthyr station with B&M locomotive No. 17 0–6–0ST alongside a TVR 0–6–2, No. 165 in 1922.   *L.C.G.B., Ken Nunn Collection*

No. 8, an 0–6–0ST shunting at Merthyr in 1922 with the TVR goods depot in the background.   *L.C.G.B., Ken Nunn Collection*

granted to sell or lease the Rumney to the Monmouthshire or the West Midland, but neither of these bigger neighbours seemed impressed; there is also a wonderful (but probably apocryphal) legend of a party of Midland Railway Directors and officers from Derby covertly inspecting the Old Rumney under the impression that it was the 'New' Rhymney Railway. Eventually and rather surprisingly, it was left to the Brecon & Merthyr to snap up the Old Rumney, under powers of 28th July, 1863, for a price not exceeding £90,000. This moderate amount may be explained by the fact that little of the modernisation envisaged by the Rumney's Act of 1861 had been carried out, and it was left to the purchaser to bear most of the expense. The same Act had given the West Midland running powers (except for traffic to the Bristol Channel ports) over the whole of the Rumney north of its inter-section by the Newport, Abergavenny & Hereford (NA&H) section of the West Midland; the connecting spur at Maesycwmmer Junction was brought into use on 28th December, 1863 by the Great Western, which by then had taken over the West Midland. On the other hand, the Brecon & Merthyr succeeded to the Rumney's valuable running powers over the Monmouth-shire (later GWR) from Bassaleg Junction into Newport.

Although later most of the traffic on the Rhymney Branch was to be coal, at the time of the purchase there were few coal mines. The Hope Pit at Cwmsyfiog was sunk by about 1830, and the New Tredegar was opened in 1853, near the hamlet of White Rose. For this colliery extensive sidings were laid in 1865 and by May 1871 White Rose station was opened. There was however little large scale development until the Elliot pits began to be sunk in 1885. These were followed in 1891 by Tredegar Ironwork's great new pit at Abertysswg, named after the Chairman, Charles McLaren: from here a tunnel ran through the mountain to the Bedwellty Colliery in the Sirhowy Valley. Later McLaren's No. 2 was opened at Pwll-Llaca. The Maerdy Pit, which lay just north of the Rhymney (Lower) station, was opened in 1876 ·but closed in 1925.

Conversion of the Old Rumney involved relaying the greater part of the line, straightening many sharp curves, and a subsequent major diversion at the Rising Sun (Graigyrhacca Curve). It nevertheless left a number of severe speed restrictions, including several to 15 mph. Partly owing to the impov-erished state of the B&M, and partly owing to the need to continue coal traffic during the alterations, it also proved a slow business. The Board of Trade Inspecting Officer twice went over the line in 1865, but on each occasion he declined to pass it for passenger traffic until further improve-ments had been carried out. Eventually, after a third inspection on 7th June, 1865, Captain Rich allowed passenger traffic to begin a week later over the 17 miles between Pengam and Newport (Dock Street). Three trains ran each way on weekdays and two on Sundays. This service was extended from Pengam to Rhymney on 16th April, 1866 (with horse-bus connection to Dowlais), and in the following year the B&M was allowed to work coal traffic from the Rhymney Valley through to Newport in train loads of not less than 120 tons.

Upon completion of the line to Rhymney, the intermediate stations were Bassaleg, Rhiwderin, Church Road, Machen, Bedwas (for Caerphilly),

A fine broadside view of 0-6-0T No. 31, seen here on 2nd August, 1905 at Newport.
L.C.G.B., Ken Nunn Collection

No. 1677 (ex No. 20 B&M) seen here in 1922 standing at Merthyr station.
L.C.G.B., Ken Nunn Collection

Maesycwmmer, Pengam, Bargoed, and New Tredegar. The only subsequent additions, other than colliery platforms, were Abertysswg (1905), Cwmsyfiog (1908), and Trethomas (1915); all these were due to colliery developments, which also caused several slight alterations to be made in the siting of some of the stations. Pengam was Fleur-de-lis until the provision of the separate platform of that name (locally, 'Flower'), while New Tredegar underwent several successive changes of name to Whiterose, Whiterose & New Tredegar, and (a rose by any other name apparently being as white) to New Tredegar & Whiterose. Bargoed became Aberbargoed after the connecting up with the main line through Bargoed (Rhymney) in 1868, while efforts were made to distinguish the B&M station at Rhymney from its RR neighbour by adding various suffixes such as (B&M), (Lower), and (Pwll Uchaf).

While the Brecon & Merthyr was thus laboriously developing its Southern Section – separated as yet by some ten miles of valley and mountain moorland from the Northern Section – its struggle with the Rhymney Railway increased in bitterness and desperation. During the years 1861–4, the Rhymney was seeking to break the Taff Vale's stranglehold on access to Cardiff by promoting its own line between the latter place and Caerphilly, powerfully supported by the LNWR, which in 1862 secured a lease of the unfinished Merthyr, Tredegar & Abergavenny Railway and which in due course was to link up with the RR by means of their joint line between Nantybwch and Rhymney.

In its battle with the Taff Vale, the RR was mercilessly harried by the B&M which promoted its own line down to Cardiff and sought again to make a line from Dowlais Top to Rhymney, and so to make itself independent of the debatable ground through the Bargoed Rhymney. The climax of this battle of the valleys came in 1864, when the Rhymney and LNWR projects were countered by three separate B&M Bills embodying proposals for no fewer than 18 different railways or junctions, of which nine were authorised by Parliament and not one (with the exception of minor deviations to existing lines and a junction with the Rhymney Limestone Railway near Pantywaun) was ever built! The outcome was an agreement whereby the Brecon & Merthyr withdrew both its own scheme for a line to Cardiff and its opposition to the Rhymney company's, in return for limited running powers (which were never exercised) over the RR into Cardiff and for various traffic facilities. A new and better junction, with attendant running powers, was also agreed from the RR at Bargoed to the B&M at Aberbargoed, the dispute in the Bargoed Rhymney Valley having already been settled on the understanding that the RR would make the line between Bargoed and Deri Junction and the B&M the piece between Dowlais Top and Deri. The B&M was to have running powers for through traffic, while the Rhymney could work over four miles of the B&M north of Deri Junction for access to Fochriw Collieries and Pantywaen Junction.

While an uneasy peace thus descended upon the Rhymney Valley, fresh strife broke out over the Brecon & Merthyr's aspirations at Merthyr. One of the few B&M proposals which obtained Parliamentary approval in 1864 was for a short connection (the Ystrad Junction) from Bedwas on the Old

Rumney across the Rhymney Valley to join the NA&H section of the GWR, with running powers up to Middle Duffryn in the Aberdare Valley. The deeper significance of this scheme became apparent in 1865, when the Brecon & Merthyr applied for powers to build a 'Southern Extension' about seven miles long from Merthyr down the west bank of the River Taff to Quakers' Yard, where it was intended to join the NA&H. In conjunction with the powers already obtained in the previous year, the Southern Extension would have given the B&M a through route from Brecon and Merthyr to Newport independent of the RR, and it is not therefore surprising to find that the Rhymney, Taff Vale, and Great Western Railways (and even the Glamorganshire Canal Company) united to fight tooth and nail. Their contention that the line was impracticable reads oddly in the light of the subsequent action of the Rhymney and Great Western in building their own joint line over an almost identical alignment, while the RR also protested, with unctuous innocence, that the B&M was promoting its Southern Extension while refusing to complete its junction with the RR at Deri, although the B&M line through Dowlais Top to Deri was ready for opening and Savin's locomotives were working over it. (The Rhymney's Bargoed–Deri line had been completed in 1864, but the RR knew very well that the B&M could not open its line between Pant and Deri for public traffic until it had honoured its legal obligations to complete a Merthyr connection.)

The joint Rhymney/GWR plan mentioned above was to build a branch from near Llancaiach up the Bargoed Taff Valley to Dowlais. Powers were obtained, but it was only in 1876 that the branch was completed to Dowlais Cae Harris station. It is a difficult valley and the gradients were dreadful – but the traffic was there. The northern part followed an existing mineral tramway to a focal point where the private line threw off three cable-worked inclines, south to Penydarren pits, west to Penydarren Works, and north to the Bargoed and Penydarren inclines in Dowlais. The new branch here also turned north and passed on the east side of the Dowlais Ironworks, putting off a branch at Zig-zag Lines Junction to Dowlais Furnace Tops. Another half-mile branch from Cwm Bargoed ran back to join a B&M branch to Fochriew colliery, which left the main line half a mile north of the station.

BRECON & MERTHYR TYDFIL JUNCTION RAILWAY
COMPANY.

TEMPORARY OFFICES,.

WATTON, BRECON,

31st January, 1877.

A Company letter-heading, dated 1877 used for the temporary offices at Brecon following a fire at Free Street.

Chapter Six
Fighting the LNWR

During the period when the Merthyr and Dowlais branches were being constructed, the Brecon & Merthyr was stubbornly but not very successfully contending against the relentless westward march of the LNWR from the direction of Abergavenny. With this object the B&M had promoted various easterly extensions in the path of the LNWR towards the Sirhowy and Ebbw Valleys, but in the face of its financial troubles and of the promotion of competitive lines by the LNWR, the smaller company was forced to concede two successive agreements which eventually admitted the invader to both Dowlais and Merthyr on very favourable terms. The first agreement, ratified by the LNWR (New Lines) Act of 15th July, 1867 authorised the LNWR to make junctions with the B&M where the two railways converged at Dowlais Top and at Ivor Junction near the terminus of the B&M Dowlais branch. The local company withdrew its competing projects in return for running powers to Nantbywch and facilities to form a junction at Rhymney Bridge towards the Rhymney Railway; no regular use was made of the former, while the idea of a junction towards the RR was dropped after the LNWR, in fulfilment of its bargain, had provided an abutment (visible to this day) for a railway that was never built.

So Euston's onward progress along the Heads of the Valleys continued; it reached Rhymney Bridge in 1871, and on 1st January, 1873 passed under the B&M's main line at Dowlais Top, close to the route's maximum altitude of 1250 ft above sea level. For the time being, LNWR progress halted at Penywern Junction, whence a ¼ mile spur connected at Ivor Junction with the B&M Dowlais branch and with the private lines of the Dowlais Iron Co. This was to prove invaluable to the LNWR, not only for ordinary commercial traffic, but also for large quantities of steel railway equipment manufactured by Dowlais.

The Dowlais Top connection was used only for the exchange of goods, mineral, and occasional excursion traffic and was finally removed about 1933, but LNWR passenger trains used the B&M passenger station at Dowlais – even after the extension of the LNWR service to Merthyr in 1879 – until the opening of Dowlais (High Street) LNWR passenger station on 4th May, 1885. Freight traffic continued to pass between the MT&A route and Dowlais (Lloyd Street, B&M), however, until 22nd November, 1954, when through traffic with the north which had hitherto passed via Abergavenny was diverted via Pontsticill, Talyllyn, and Hereford.

The final chapter in the Brecon & Merthyr's struggle with the LNWR was written in 1874–79. Like the B&M before it, the larger company had tried several times to find a way down from the hilltops into Merthyr, notably in 1865 when it deposited plans for a zig-zag line from Dowlais, which would have twice crossed the fixed incline of the Dowlais Railway. Eventually in 1874 it promoted a fresh Bill for a Merthyr extension; the B&M withdrew its opposition to this, and agreed to its own Merthyr branch becoming joint with the LNWR, in consideration of the latter repaying half the cost of construction, at £25,000 a mile. In order to reach the B&M at Morlais Junction, the LNWR built an extension from Penywern Junction which

No. 2179 (ex No. 3, B&M) seen here on a long, mixed goods train near Merthyr in November 1922.   *L.C.G.B., Ken Nunn Collection*

An immaculate No. 17, 0–6–0ST on a Dowlais train seen here in September 1922 at Pant station.   *L.C.G.B., Ken Nunn Collection*

crossed under the B&M four times in 1½ miles and included a costly tunnel. The link was completed and LNWR services to Merthyr (High Street) began on 1st June, 1879, although the section between Morlais and Rhydycar Junctions had become formally vested in the two companies jointly four years previously – the LNWR was taking no chances, especially as about that time the B&M was considering selling out to the Midland Railway!

In addition to its capture of the Hereford, Hay & Brecon, the Midland Railway in the early 1870s was keenly interested in the possibilities of obtaining a through route to Newport and of forming an alliance for this purpose with the Sirhowy and the Monmouthshire Railways, both of which were as yet still independent but were the objectives of discreet approaches by both the Great Western and the London & North Western. Although the Midland dismissed the Brecon & Merthyr as '60 miles of single line unable to earn its keep', the B&M might well provide a means of enabling the Midland to reach the Sirhowy and the Monmouthshire, and in 1873 the Derby management seemed likely to get the B&M for annual payments starting at £34,500 and rising to £49,460 in the twelfth year. The Brecon Board and its ordinary shareholders were prepared to settle on these terms, but when in 1874 the Midland and the Monmouthshire jointly promoted a Bill to acquire the B&M the debenture shareholders of the Brecon company petitioned against it on the grounds that their rights would be abrogated. The Midland's withdrawal from the Bill, and its consequent collapse, meant the end of MR ambitions in South Wales, and in due course the Sirhowy and the Monmouthshire Railways passed into the control of the LNWR and the Great Western respectively.

By this time about 25 passenger trains a day were using the four miles of single line and tunnel between Brecon and Talyllyn, and this number would have been still greater had various schemes for railway communication between Abergavenny and Brecon come to fruition. The Vale of Crickhowell Railway, incorporated in 1864 to connect the MT&A Railway near Abergavenny with Crickhowell, promoted a further Bill in 1866 to extend this scheme for 14 miles from Crickhowell to join the Neath & Brecon immediately east of Mount Street. To this projected invasion the Brecon & Merthyr reacted with customary briskness by promoting its own line from Talyllyn to Abergavenny, which it withdrew on securing an agreement (confirmed by the Vale of Crickhowell Act of 1866) that the latter's line would not be made west of Talybont, in return for running powers over the B&M thence to Brecon, the B&M also to double its line between Talybont and Brecon, except through the tunnel. Readers who have followed the fortunes of our hero so far will not be surprised to learn that none of these plans ever came to anything and that a subsequent Usk Valley Railway Company, incorporated in 1898 to make a railway from Abergavenny to Talyllyn, proved equally abortive. So the most suitable physical approach to Brecon was never actually used by a railway.

Fowler 0−6−0ST No. 13 (built in 1886, this locomotive was withdrawn in 1923 carrying the GWR No. 2185) on a goods train near Rhydycar Junction. For some years prior to the grouping this locomotive was the only one allocated to Talyllyn.
L.C.G.B., Ken Nunn Collection

Fowler 0−6−0ST No. 14 heads a goods train between Merthyr and Cefn. Built at the same time as sister engine No. 13 (*above*), she lasted several years longer, until 1934 (GWR No. 2186).
L.C.G.B., Ken Nunn Collection

Chapter Seven

The Pontypridd, Caerphilly & Newport Railway

The next contentious chapter in B&M history centred round the Machen—Caerphilly branch, which had been authorised by the Old Rumney's Act of 1861 and constructed under the supervision of the latter's Engineer, Brewer, following the B&M's acquisition of the Old Rumney. Save for the bridge over the Rhymney River it was an unpretentious single-track affair extending 3¾ miles to an end-on junction with the Rhymney Railway half a mile east of the present Caerphilly station; opened without ceremony in 1864, it was at first little more than a glorified siding serving local collieries and works. Its strategic implications were fleetingly recognised during the 'war' with the RR when the B&M sought to make it a spring-board towards Cardiff, but it was left to a third party to turn it to important account.

This was the Pontypridd, Caerphilly & Newport Railway (PC&N), incorporated on 8th August, 1878 with the powerful support of the Alexandra (Newport) Dock Company and of certain influential colliery proprietors in Glamorganshire, with the dual object of developing Newport as a coal-shipping port in competition with the Cardiff—Penarth monopoly; and of avoiding the 'Park Mile' between Bassaleg and Park Junction, with its onerous tolls on coal traffic bound for Newport. The latter object was never realised (although the tolls were in due course bought out), but agreements for traffic facilities were obtained with the Taff Vale, Rhymney, and B&M Railways; the last named decided in 1882 to double its line between Bassaleg and Machen (and, incidentally, on to Abertysswg) in anticipation of greatly increased traffic.

No agreement appears to have been sought with the Great Western for running powers over the Park Mile, however, and when on 7th July, 1884 the inaugural coal train set out from Pontypridd for Newport behind a Taff Vale engine, it was evidently considered that east of Bassaleg the Brecon & Merthyr's running powers would suffice. At Caerphilly a B&M pilot engine was coupled in front, no doubt with the object of lending an air of legality to the subsequent proceedings as well as of helping the Taff Vale engine up the 1 in 39 into Machen. Neither this device nor the production by Alfred Henshaw, the Brecon & Merthyr's traffic manager, of a 'permit to proceed', proved satisfactory, however, to a Great Western reception committee at Bassaleg Junction; the signals remained at danger, and the frustrated celebrants put their train in the loop, sent the engines back light, and dispersed to await the outcome of a telegram to Paddington. Nearly three weeks later the Great Western decided it could not or would not oppose the entry of the PC&N and a substantial and increasing mineral traffic began.

By this time the PC&N had become virtually consolidated with the Alexandra (Newport & South Wales) Docks and Railway Company (AD&R), created in 1882 as a reconstitution of the Alexandra (Newport) Dock Company, although it was not until 1897 that the PC&N was formally absorbed. In 1883 the AD&R obtained powers to construct a new double line, parallel with the Great Western and subject to the same tolls, from the Brecon & Merthyr immediately east of Bassaleg and along the Park Mile to the existing dock lines, and this was opened in April 1886. The Taff Vale continued to work the Pontypridd coal trains until 30th April, 1906, when the AD&R provided its own power; while the Brecon & Merthyr worked coal trains from the Old Rumney section through to Newport Docks. On the Machen–Caerphilly branch proper the traffic working was even more complicated. Passenger services were begun in 1887 and worked variously by the AD&R, Great Western, and Rhymney Railways, the only non-participant being the Brecon & Merthyr (the owning company), which contented itself with the local goods traffic.

From the opening of this route, the steep climb from the river bank up to Machen was a source of difficulty in working the coal traffic, and in 1887 the PC&N Company obtained powers for the Machen Loop Line, diverging from the original branch at Gwaunybara Junction (about halfway between Caerphilly and Machen) then climbing away on its north side across the river at a ruling gradient of 1 in 200 to join the B&M main line at Machen. This loop was brought into use on 14th September, 1891 and was later transferred to the B&M in consideration of the AD&R being paid in per-petuity half the gross receipts from the Caerphilly branch.

The existence of these separate up (westbound) and down (eastbound) lines led to a curious situation when halts were provided for the rail-motors, at White Hart (Machen), Waterloo, Fountain Bridge, and Gwernydomen. The first- and last-named enjoyed train service in both directions, White Hart (opened as late as 1947) having platforms on both lines but separated by a road; Waterloo and Fountain Bridge, however, were served by trains in one direction only – up and down respectively. The life of White Hart Halt was exceptionally short; it was closed on 30th June, 1952.

Last entrant into the South Wales railway network and into B&M territory was the Barry Railway (ByR), which in 1898 obtained powers to extend from Penrhos Lower Junction into and across the Rhymney Valley to join the B&M 1¼ miles above Bedwas at 'Barry Junction (B&M)', Duffryn Isaf. By means of this connection, which was brought into use 2nd January, 1905, and by running powers right up to Rhymney, the Barry was able to attract considerable coal traffic from the upper part of the Rhymney Valley, but its running powers were for minerals only, and merchandise was either exchanged at Duffryn Isaf or worked by B&M engines across the huge Llanbradach Viaduct of the ByR to Energlyn Junction on the west side of the valley. No regular passenger trains used this route, but seasonal excursions were run to Barry Island; after grouping the connection became redundant, the whole 3¾ mile branch being closed. Llanbradach viaduct however was not demolished until 1937.

Not content with this penetration of the Rhymney Valley, the Barry Railway in 1905 and succeeding years fought vigorously to secure entry into both the Bargoed Rhymney and into the Western Valleys of Monmouthshire. The former project, which failed in 1906, was for a line just over two miles long, from the B&M south of Aberbargoed to pass above the RR main line north of Bargoed, enter the Bargoed Rhymney valley, and bypass the Groesfaen defile by a tunnel 220 yds long. It would then have passed up the east side of the valley on gradients of 1 in 43–48 to join the B&M north of Deri Junction.

The Brecon & Merthyr itself had been first in the field, as early as 1865, in supporting an 'Ebbw Vale & Cardiff Junction Railway' (for which the Engineer was our old friend Conybeare), which by means of a triangular junction at Machen and a long tunnel thence through the intervening mountain would have led into the Sirhowy Valley at Nine Mile Point and so to the Western Valleys line of the Monmouthshire Railway above Cross Keys. On and off for the next 40 years, the same battle-ground was fought over by the Rhymney, London & North Western, Great Western, Brecon & Merthyr, and lastly the Barry. Every one of these schemes would have involved crossing over or connecting with the B&M between Caerphilly and Machen, but in the end no such line was ever made, even though in 1907, the B&M having withdrawn its own Bill, the Barry Railway one was finally passed.

Although the B&M played only a minor part in the attempt in the mid-eighties by Sir Edward Watkin, the energetic and controversial Chairman of the Manchester Sheffield & Lincolnshire Railway (MS&L), to build an empire from the Mersey to the Bristol Channel, some details must be told. It was of course a revival of earlier schemes, and secured an Act as the Welsh Union Railway. In 1889 Watkin became Chairman of the Neath & Brecon Railway; he also steered through Parliament the Welsh Railways Through Traffic Bill, in which the MS&L, Cheshire Lines and twelve Welsh railways were joined, as well as being very busy promoting new lines up in the Wirral. Watkin had two choices for reaching the South Wales ports; one via the B&M to Newport, the other by way of the Neath & Brecon to Swansea. However, the latter route was in the hands of the Midland Railway. Now came the drama; the Agreement whereby the Midland worked the N&B line from Brecon to Ynysygeinon Junction came up for renewal, and Watkin made the new terms so onerous that the Midland had no option but to announce, on 1st July, 1889 that it would withdraw all trains between Brecon and Swansea. After a short stalemate, by 6th July the N&B had borrowed enough MS&L stock to restart a service, but it was a disaster. The N&B simply was not able to more than double its train services at a stroke. Negotiations followed, and by 22nd July the Midland trains were back at Brecon, but only by virtue of running powers, not as leaseholders.

Meanwhile, Watkin had got heavily involved in his Manchester to Paris Railway, for which purpose he had bought the South Eastern and Metropolitan Railways and planned the Great Central, and the Welsh Union Railway seems to have taken a back seat. Although finally by new construction to the north it did become possible to run trains from South Wales to Birkenhead without the help of either the GWR or LNWR, the steam had gone out of the scheme, and the prospect of major express trains trying to climb the B&M's famous Seven Mile Bank had faded.

No. 48 0–6–2T taking on water at Pant station, before leaving on a local service in August 1922.   *L.C.G.B., Ken Nunn Collection*

Talybont station as photographed in July 1904 showing the substantial station buildings, water tower and most unusual stone water column.   *Locomotive Publishing Co.*

Chapter Eight
Modest Prosperity

In the first two decades of the present century, the Brecon & Merthyr Railway enjoyed an era which, by comparison with the greater part of its previous history, was one of relative prosperity. After further capital reconstructions in 1882 and 1902, interest was regularly paid on the preference stocks, and in the closing years 1918–21 the full dividend of 4 per cent was met on both first and second preference stocks. Although the company's final year, 1921, was affected by three months of the national coal strike, net receipts of over £67,000 were earned, in relation to capital of £2,075,581. Total traffic conveyed over the line was about 2½ million passengers and four million tons of freight traffic, principally coal. Track mileage totalled 82 m. 44 ch., of which 59 m. 66 ch. represented first track, 20 m. 41 ch. double track, 1 m. 17 ch. third track, and precisely one mile fourth track, the last-named comprising up and down running loops between Trethomas and Bedwas.

An Act of 1892 fixed new maximum charges for freight for the B&M; it was a run-of-the-mill Act, but interesting because to save time Parliament extended it to cover some other railways, including the Llanelly & Mynydd Mawr, which only carried coal, and the Ravenglass & Eskdale which hardly carried anything. The list was in great detail, including a rate for carrying 'cork socks'. An Act of 1895 enabled further money to be raised. Yet another Act of some interest was passed in 1914; this permitted extra land to be purchased at Machen Works and elsewhere and also sorted out some difficulties with the Rhymney Railway over running powers. It somewhat relaxed the rules about what the B&M could carry over the Rhymney between Deri Junction and Bargoed, and gave it running powers to Adam Street goods station in Cardiff, with some restrictions. The Rhymney's powers, granted in 1863, to work traffic over the B&M to 'any works of the Dowlais Iron Co. in the vicinity of Dowlais Big Pond' was amended to read 'any works of Guest Keen & Nettlefolds'. The main purpose was to retain access to Fochriew Colliery, but there were others close by.

In 1908 the B&M announced that in the six months to June 30th it carried 401,023 passengers; however 76,044 were in trains of other companies; these figures may perhaps include the 'Cambrian' trains from Merthyr to Aberystwyth.

One of the final acts in the competitive period in South Wales was yet another attempt (by the Alexandra Docks Railway) to make a connection with the LNWR in the Sirhowy Valley. This would have required a junction with the B&M at Bassaleg and a run up the west side of Ebbw Vale to Nine Mile Point. Acts were obtained in 1911 and 1914, but the War finished off the scheme.

During its lifetime the B&M had seven Chairmen, but only three traffic (later general) managers: Alfred Henshaw (1863–94), John Gall (1894–1903), and Herbert R. Price (1903–22). The first Chairman, and virtual 'father' of the undertaking, John Parry de Winton, was in office from 1859 until his death in November 1864, at the age of 86. The association between the de Winton family and the railway went on for nearly half a century longer, however, as the family firm of Wilkins & Co., Brecon, continued as bankers to the company until taken over by Lloyds Bank in 1890. William de Winton, the eldest surviving son of J.P., joined the B&M Board in the year of his father's death and continued a member until he died in 1907, at the age of 84. Henry, another son of J.P., was also a Director from 1862 to 1868.

After the Railways Act of 1921, the Brecon & Merthyr was absorbed as a subsidiary company of the Western Group (GWR) on and from 1st July, 1922. The last Chairman was Sir George Pigot, Bart., while the Board included several names famous in South Wales industrial history; the Earl of Bessborough (whose family was related by marriage to the Guests of Dowlais), Lord Tredegar, and Major David Davies, M.P. (afterwards Lord Davies), grandson of 'Dai Davies the Ocean', who had helped to inspire the Brecon & Merthyr Railway.

The Headquarters Offices of the Brecon & Merthyr Railway – Tredegar Chambers – Newport. *Courtesy, GWR Magazine*

Chapter Nine
Working the Railway

The Brecon & Merthyr had two over-riding problems when it came to operating the trains. One was shared with all Welsh railways; severe gradients. This brought speed restrictions, short goods trains, much use of banking engines, and not a few mishaps. The other was the complexity of junctions and industrial sidings In the south, shared by most of its neighbours there; however, it would not have wished it otherwise, for they all brought in revenue, which the seven mile bank at Torpantau certainly did not.

During the latter part of the last century, there were also severe weather conditions in winter; successive generations of railwaymen nevertheless responded to this challenge, to endow the old B&M with a standard of safety which must be considered very good in such conditions, and with a tradition of comradeship which became almost legendary in the South Wales valleys.

Running the traffic in the old days must have been both hard and hazardous, but the growth of the Newport coal trade towards the end of last century enabled a programme of modernisation to be carried out. Apart from doubling the track nearly all the way from Bassaleg to Rhymney, the electric train token system was introduced on all single line sections except between Morlais Junction and Rhydycar Junction, where the electric train staff was used. Tyer's block telegraph system was employed on the double line sections and McKenzie & Holland's type of somersault signal was made standard. An unusual, but not unique, feature of B&M signalling was that certain distant signals on steep falling gradients were to be treated as 'stop' signals if the semaphore was in the 'on' position. During the years 1903–14 most of the track was relaid with 80 lb. and 90 lb. rails, enabling some easement to be made in the overall speed restrictions of 25 mph for passenger trains and 14 mph for goods trains, subject to much stricter limits at many intermediate places. In accordance with South Wales tradition B&M 'up' trains were those going up the valleys and 'down' trains those coming down to the seaboard.

Brecon & Merthyr quarter-mile posts were white with one to three black bands. Station name boards were salmon pink with black lettering; the upper part of signal boxes were also salmon pink. The line excluding sidings comprised at its peak 25¼ miles of double track and 36½ of single.

As previously stated, the first timetables showed only two trains per day from Brecon to Pant. These were so timed that one train could cover the service, leaving 'Dowlais' about 9 am and returning from the second trip at 6.15 pm. The Mid-Wales Railway showed trains to all stations between Talyllyn and Dowlais (and later Merthyr) as if they were its own; no doubt more passengers wished to visit South Wales than those wanting to go to Brecon. Through trains or carriages from Dowlais to Aberystwyth via the Mid-Wales seem to have begun in 1865; certainly these were regular as soon as the line was open to Merthyr. On these trains, and of course Mid-Wales trains from Brecon to Llanidloes, passengers could change at Llechryd (Builth Road) on to the LNWR-controlled Central Wales Railway; one train gave immediate connection there to an LNW one comprising through carriages to Manchester, Liverpool, Edinburgh and other towns. At Brecon advertisements promised 'Brecon to Manchester (and other towns) with only one change of carriage'. For the wealthy, travelling with much baggage, this was an important facility; it was not one that the B&M's run-of-the-mill passengers needed, but this link between the industrial area of South Wales with that of the North of England must have been welcome to the fast-rising class of engineers and entrepreneurs.

At the southern end, there was a change of terminus in 1880, when the B&M trains began to run into High Street station at Newport instead of Dock Street. This station, reached by a new spur from Park Junction, was progressively improved, notably in 1936 apart from the reconstruction of 1880 to accommodate trains from the Eastern and Western Valleys lines of the Monmouthshire Railway (absorbed by the GWR in that year) as well as those of the B&M.

The accident of history whereby the 'Brecon' and 'Rumney' lines remained disconnected until 1868 was reflected in their operation as two distinct sections, designated as such in the working timetables, while locomotives and passenger train-sets remained almost permanently allocated to the respective sections. Nor was there any great change during the company's history in the pattern of the passenger services, which for generations were something of a popular byword for sloth and unpunctuality. In her 'Country Book', *Monmouthshire*, Olive Phillips recalls that 'any slow train is affectionately called "The Brecon & Merthyr" in these parts', while any Edwardian music-hall comic who got a laugh with a slow-train joke at Boscombe or Bath would make a mental note to trot it out when next playing at Newport Lyceum – merely changing the name of the railway from Somerset & Dorset to Brecon & Merthyr.

Apart from the physical difficulties already referred to, however, it was no easy task for the B&M to run its main line service to time, considering that the trains were dependent upon other companies' connections at both ends, upon its own or other branch connections at six intermediate junctions, and upon the favour of the Rhymney and Great Western Railways, whose tracks were used in the middle and at the Newport end of the through journey respectively. All these things considered, the B&M did very well.

The basis of the 'main line' service had always been either three or four trains each weekday from Newport to Brecon and vice versa, the overall journey times ranging from just over 2¼ hours to nearly three hours; in the summer of 1914, the afternoon departure from Newport called at Bassaleg, Church Road, and Rhiwderin 'to set down from London, on notice being given to the guard', and managed the Newport–Brecon journey of 47 miles in 2 hrs 18 mins. Merthyr and Dowlais connections were normally made at Pontsticill and Pant respectively, except that until World War I the midday train from Brecon was formed of portions for both Merthyr and Newport, the engines for both destinations double-heading the cavalcade as far as Pontsticill; the Dowlais connection with this train, and with its balancing up service, was also made by extending the Dowlais branch train to Pontsticill. Public Sunday services were run in the early years but were soon discontinued, although colliers' trains continued to run if required in connection with shifts starting or finishing on the Sabbath.

recon, Merthyr, and Newport.]   **[Brecon & Merthyr.**

BREOON, MERTHYR, DOWLAIS, RHYMNEY, and NEWPORT.—Brecon and Merthyr.
Sec. and Gen. Man., H. K. Price, Newport (Mon.)

Down.   Week Days.

New Joint Station,	mrn	mrn	mrn	mrn	non	aft	aft	aft	aft	aft	aft	aft		
Brecon ....dep.	....	7 45	....	....	12 0	....	2 5		....	5 10	....			
Talyllyn Junction	....	7 59	....	....	1215	....	2 30		....	5 30	....			
Talybont-on-Usk	....	8 9	....	....	1225	....	2 40		....	5 40	....			
Torpantau	....	8 29	....	....	1245	....	3 0		....	6 0	....			
Dolygaer	....	8 33	....	....	1250	....	3 6		....	6 4	....			
Pontsticill Junction	....	8 37	....	....	1254	....	3 10		....	6 8	....			
Pontsticill Junction ...dep.	....	8 50	1010	....	1 0	....	3 20		....	6 22	7 55			
Pontsarn, for Vaynor	....	8 55	1016	....	1 5	....	3 25		....	6 28	8 1			
Cefn	....	9 2	1021	....	1 19	....	3 32		....	6 35	8 10			
Merthyr 67, 71, 109. arr.	....	9 12	1030	....	1 28	....	3 40		....	6 45	8 20			
Pant Junction	....	8 45	....	....	1 7	....	3 28	4 3	....	6 25	....	1024		
464 Dowlais {arr.	....	9 0	....	....	1 12	....	3 43	....	....	6 25	....	....		
{dep.	....	8 35	....	....	....	....	3 20	3 55	....	6 10	....	1015		
Dowlais Top	....	8 52	....	....	....	....	3 38	4 9	....	6 24	....	1029		
Fochriw	....	8 59	....	....	....	....	3 45	4 17	....	6 31	....	1037		
Darran and Deri	....	9 5	....	....	....	....	3 51	4 24	....	6 37	....	1044		
Bargoed Junction 470	....	9 15	....	....	....	....	3 58	4 33	....	6 47	....	1053		
Mls Rhymney & Pont- dep.	7 50	8 45	....	1130	....	2 55	....	....	6 10	....	8 0			
1 Abertysswg ....[lottyn	7 53	8 48	....	1133	....	2 58	....	....	6 13	....	8 3			
2½ New Tredegar *	7 57	8 52	....	1137	....	3 2	....	....	6 17	....	8 7			
3½ Cwmsyfiog and Brithdir	8 0	8 55	....	1140	....	3 5	....	....	6 20	....	8 10			
4½ Bargoed & Aberbargoed	8 3	8 58	....	1144	....	3 8	....	....	6 23	....	8 13			
5 Pengam † (below)... arr.	8 6	9 1	....	1147	....	3 11	....	....	6 26	....	8 16			
Pengam † (below)	....	8 7	9 20	....	1148	....	3 13	4 54	40 6 27	6 53	....	8 17	11 0	
Maesycwmmer and Hengoed	....	8 12	9 24	....	1153	....	3 18	4 10	....	6 32	6 58	....	8 21	
Bedwas	....	8 22	9 33	....	12 3	....	3 27	4 19	....	....	7 7	....	8 30	
Machen 67	....	8 29	9 39	....	1210	....	3 33	4 27	....	....	7 14	....	8 36	
Church Road	....	8 34	9 43	....	1215	....	3 37	4 32	....	....	7 19	....	8 40	
Rhiwderin	....	8 39	9 47	....	1221	....	3 42	4 37	....	....	7 24	....	8 44	
Bassaleg 67	....	8 46	9 56	....	1231	....	3 49	4 45	....	....	7 34	....	8 50	
Newport(HighSt)55, 62 arr.	....	8 55	10 5	....	1240	....	3 58	4 55	....	....	7 45	....	9 0	

Up.   Week Days.

High Street Station,	mrn	mrn	aft	aft	aft	aft	aft	aft	a	aft				
Newport ....dep.	8 25	1010	....	1 10	2 17	....	4 45	....	6 15	1010	....			
Bassaleg	8 34	1019	....	1 19	2 26	....	4 53	....	6 24	1010	....			
Rhiwderin	8 38	1023	....	1 23	2 30	....	4 57	....	6 28	1014	....			
Church Road	8 43	1028	....	1 28	2 35	....	5 2	....	6 33	1019	....			
Machen 470	8 47	1032	....	1 32	2 39	....	5 6	....	6 37	1024	....			
Bedwas	8 54	1039	....	1 39	2 46	....	5 13	....	6 44	1032	....			
Maesycwmmer and Hengoed	9 3	1048	....	1 48	2 55	....	5 22	....	6 53	1042	....			
Pengam and Fleur-de-lis..	9 8	1053	....	1 53	3 0	....	5 27	5 32	6 58	1047	....			
Pengam & Fleur-de-lis dep.	9 25	1056	....	1 56	....	....	5 29	....	7 10	1050	....			
Bargoed and Aberbargoed	9 29	11 0	....	2 1	....	....	5 34	....	7 15	1055	....			
Cwmsyfiog and Brithdir..	9 33	11 4	....	2 5	....	....	5 37	....	7 18	1059	....			
New Tredegar and Tirphil.	9 37	11 8	....	2 10	....	....	5 41	....	7 22	11 4	....			
Abertysswg {470	9 42	1113	....	2 14	....	....	5 46	....	7 27	11 9	....			
Rhymney & Pontlottyn a	9 45	1116	....	2 17	....	....	5 49	....	7 30	1112	....			
Bargoed Junction 470	9 27	....	....	3 9	....	....	5 37	7 7	1114	....				
Darran and Deri	9 33	....	....	3 15	....	....	5 43	7 13	1120	....				
Fochriw	9 41	....	....	3 23	....	....	5 51	7 21	1128	....				
Dowlais Top	9 48	....	....	3 29	....	....	5 58	7 28	1135	....				
464 Dowlais {arr.	10 5	....	....	....	3 43	....	....	6 8	7 40	1145				
{dep.	9 40	....	....	1215	3 20	....	....	7 25	....	....				
Pant Junction	9 55	....	1220	....	3 35	....	....	6 2	7 35	1189				
Mls Merthyr ....dep.	9 38	....	1210	....	2 50	5 30	....	....	7 15	....				
2½ Cefn	9 47	....	1220	....	3 5	5 40	....	....	7 25	....				
4½ Pontsarn, for Vaynor ..	9 52	....	1225	....	3 15	5 45	....	....	7 30	....				
6½ Pontsticill Junc. (above)	9 56	....	1230	....	3 11	5 50	....	....	7 35	....				
Pontsticill Junction (above)	10 3	....	1235	....	3 40	....	....	7 44	....	....				
Dolygaer	10 7	....	1240	....	3 44	....	....	7 48	....	....				
Torpantau	1012	....	1245	....	3 49	....	....	7 53	....	....				
Talybont-on-Usk	1032	....	....	....	4 9	....	....	8 13	....	....				
Talyllyn Junction 468, 625	1040	....	1 13	....	4 17	....	....	8 21	....	....				
Brecon 625 ....arr.	11 0	....	1 40	....	4 30	....	....	8 35	....	....				

NOTES.

a Stops at **Pentir Rhiw**, between Torpantau and Talybont-on-Usk, to set down on notice being given to the Station Master at Pontsticill, Dolygaer, or Torpantau.

* New Tredegar and Tirphil.

† Pengam and Fleur-de-lis.

☞ For OTHER TRAINS BETWEEN PAGE **Machen** and **Newport** 67

Bradshaw's passenger timetable for April 1910.

The Brecon & Merthyr also participated in the working of relatively long-distance summer holiday traffic between the South Wales industrial centres and the Central Wales spas and Aberystwyth. Special provision was first made for this traffic in 1891, by an 11.10 am train from Newport which made its first stop at Pengam and connected at Talyllyn with a Mid-Wales train from Brecon to Aberystwyth. From this beginning there developed seasonal through services from Cardiff (Rhymney) via Bargoed and from Cardiff (Queen Street) and the Rhondda Valley via Merthyr; a through service between Barry and Llandrindod Wells was added much later, after the local companies became part of the GWR. All these trains used the East Loop at Talyllyn and in pre-grouping days changed engines at No. 1 Box, except that during the early 1900s a Cambrian 4-4-0 was stationed at Merthyr specially for the purpose of working through to Aberystwyth the Cardiff train, the RR and TVR portions of which were combined at Pontsticill. This involved the unusual arrangement of an engine having to turn (at Moat Lane) midway through its journey. By 1908 the Taff Vale was providing the motive power over the B&M while on the resumption of the services after World War I, and until 1921, the Rhondda Valley train was worked through to Talyllyn by a TVR 0-6-2T and men from Treherbert shed, who 'ran round' their train at both Pontypridd and Merthyr.

There was a competing route from South Wales to Aberystwyth via the Manchester & Milford Railway (M&M), which was in the hands of the Great Western from 1906. In 1920 a seasonal Monday, Saturday, Sunday-only service was begun by this route, which cut the Cambrian out but did not entirely fail to benefit the B&M, as the train used it between Bassaleg and Caerphilly, and pieces of five other companies' lines before arriving on M&M metals at Pencader Junction.

On the Caerphilly branch the services were complex. On 28th December, 1887 a service was begun from Newport to Pontypridd via Caerphilly, worked by the Alexandra Docks & Railway Co. whose line joined the B&M just east of Bassaleg, and left it at Penrhos Junction west of Caerphilly. However this service was taken over by the Great Western in 1899; between Machen and Pontypridd most trains stopped only at Caerphilly. In 1904 the AD&R began a steam railcar service from Pontypridd to Caerphilly, and from 1908 the Rhymney Railway operated a steam railcar between Senghenydd and Machen via Caerphilly. All the South Wales railways, with the exception of the B&M were bitten by the steam railcar bug, ardently advocated by Mr Hurry Riches of the Taff Vale. The two AD&R steam railcars were designed by Dugald Drummond of the LSWR, another strong advocate of railcars; No. 1 (58 ft 4 in. long) entered service on 1st September, 1904, and the second (64 ft 11 in.) on 28th September. However neither the AD&R nor Rhymney cars were a great success; by 1917 when the AD&R put on a through Pontypridd–Machen service, both steam railcars were out of use. After the War, the Great Western ran a service from Newport to Pontypridd via Caerphilly.

The Rhymney branch service, amounting at its peak to about eight trains a day each way between Newport and Rhymney, was conducted as an entirely separate entity except that one or two trains started from or terminated at

Brecon, Merthyr, Dowlais, Rhymney, and Newport.

BRECON, MERTHYR, DOWLAIS, RHYMNEY, and NEWPORT.—G.W. (late Brecon and Merthyr).

Down. — Week Days only.

Miles	Down.	mrn	mrn	mrn	mrn	mrn	aft	non	aft	aft	aft	aft	aft	aft	aft	aft	aft
	Brecon .... dep.	....	....	7 35	....	....	....	12 0	Runs to Dowlais, arr. at 1 19 aft., *see below.*	2 5	....	....	....	Mons. & Sats.	5 45	....	....
4¼	Talyllyn Junction .... arr.	....	....	7 45	....	....	....	12 10		2 15	....	....	....		5 53	....	....
	Talyllyn Junction .... dep.	....	....	7 50	....	....	....	12 15		2 30	....	....	....		6 5	....	Saturdays only.
7	Talybont-on-Usk	....	....	8 2	....	....	....	12 25		2 40	....	....	....		6 15	....	
—	Pentir Rhiw	....	....	8s14	....	....	....	....		2t50	....	....	....		6a27	....	
14¼	Torpantau	....	....	8 25	....	....	....	12 47		3 2	....	....	....		6 38	....	
15¾	Dolygaer	....	....	8 29	....	....	....	12 51		3 6	....	....	....		6 42	....	
17¼	Pontsticill Junction .... arr.	....	....	8 33	....	....	....	12 55		3 10	....	....	....	5 5	6 46	....	
—	Pontsticill Junction .. dep.	....	....	8 50	....	1015	....	1 19		3 20	....	....	....	5 8	7 10	....	
20	Pontsarn, for Vaynor	....	....	8 55	....	1021	....	1 24		3 25	....	....	....	....	7 15	....	
21½	Cefn Coed	....	....	9 6	....	1026	....	1 32		3 32	....	....	....	5 21	7 25	....	
24¼	Merthyr 92, 111, 115 arr.	....	....	9 16	....	1035	....	1 40		3 40	....	....	....	5 30	7 35	....	
—	Pontsticill Junction .... dep.	....	....	8 39	....	Stop	....	1 4	1 9	3 24	....	....	5A25	Through Train from Aberystwyth (dep. 12 15 aft.) via Builth Wells and Talyllyn, see pages 580 & 582.	6 55	....	....
19	Pant *(below)* .... arr.	....	....	8 43	....		....	1 8	1 13	3 28	....	....	5A29		6 59	....	....
—	Mls Dowlais .... dep.	....	....	8 30	9 40	....	Saturdays only.	11A50	Stop	3 20	4 0	4s40	....		6 45	7 50	9 15
—	¾ Pantysgallog	....	....	8 33	9 43	....		11A53		3 23	4 3	4s43	....		6 48	7 53	9 18
—	1¼ Pant *(below)* .... arr.	....	....	8 35	9 45	....		11A55	....	3 25	4 5	4s45	....		6 50	7 55	9 20
—	Pant .... dep.	....	....	8 45	Stop	....		1 10	....	3 33	...	4s49	5A30		7 1	Stop	9 25
20½	Dowlais Top ‡	....	....	8 51		....		1 16	....	3 38	...	4s54	5A35		7 6		9 30
23½	Fochriw	....	....	8 58	....	....		1 23	....	3 45	...	5s1	5 42		7 13	....	9 38
26¼	Darran and Deri	....	....	9 4	....	....		1 29	....	3 51	...	5s7	5 48		7 19	....	9 45
28¼	Bargoed Junction 111	....	....	9 15	....	....		1 36	....	3 58	...	5s15	5 54		7 28	. .	9 54
30	Pengam † *(below)* .... arr.	....	....	9 19	mrn	mrn		1 40	aft	4 3	...	5s20	....		7 34	aft	....
—	Mls Rhymney & Pontlottyn dep.	7 45	8 35	....	1015	1120	1 19	....	2 55	....	....	5 27	....		....	6 40	....
—	1 Abertysswg	7 48	8 38	....	1018	1123	1 22	....	2 58	....	....	5 30	....		....	6 43	....
—	2½ New Tredegar *	7 53	8 43	....	1023	1128	1 26	....	3 2	....	....	5 34	....		....	6 47	....
—	3¼ Cwmsyfiog and Brithdir	7 56	8 46	....	1026	1131	1 29	....	3 5	....	....	5 37	....		....	6 50	....
—	4¼ Bargoed & Aberbargoed	8 0	8 50	....	1030	1135	1 32	....	3 8	....	....	5 40	....		....	6 53	....
—	5 Pengam † *(below)* ... arr.	8 3	8 54	....	1034	1138	1 35	....	3 11	....	....	5 43	....		....	6 56	....
—	Pengam & Fleur-de-lis .. dep.	8 5	8 55	9 21	1036	1140	....	1 42	3 13	4 5	...	5 44	....		7 37	6 57	....
31¾	Maesycwmmer and Hengoed	8 10	9 0	9 26	1041	1145	....	1 47	3 18	4 10	...	5 49	....		7 42	7 3	....
36½	Bedwas	8 19	....	9 35	1050	1154	....	1s56	3 23	4 19	...	5 58	....		7 52	—	....
—	Trethomas	8 22	....	....	1053	1157	....	1s59	3 31	....	...	6 1	....		7s56	....	....
39½	Machen 109	8 27	....	9 42	1058	12 2	....	2s4	3 35	4 27	...	6 5	....		8 0	....	....
40¾	Church Road	8 32	....	9 46	11 3	12 7	....	2s8	3 40	4 31	...	6 10	....		8 5	....	....
43	Rhiwderin	8 37	....	9 50	11 8	1211	....	2s12	3 45	4 36	...	6 15	....		8 11	....	....
44	Bassaleg ‖	8 45	....	10 1	1116	1219	....	2s17	3 53	4 45	...	6 25	....		8 23	....	....
47	Newport 60, 65, 74, 102 arr.	8 55	....	1010	1125	1228	....	2s26	4 3	4 58	...	6 35	....		8 33	....	....

Up. — Week Days only.

Miles	Up.	mrn	mrn	mrn	mrn	mrn	mrn	aft	aft	aft	aft	aft	aft	aft	aft	aft	aft
	Newport .... dep.	...	8 25	9 45	Through Train to Aberystwyth (arr. 5 aft.) via Talyllyn and Builth Wells, see pages 582 and 578.	....	1155	1 5	2 45	....	....	4 50	....	...	6 25	9 10	....
3	Bassaleg ‖	...	8 34	9 55		....	12 4	1 14	2 55	....	....	4 59	....	...	6 35	9 20	....
4	Rhiwderin	...	8 38	10 0		....	12 8	1 18	3 0	....	....	5 3	....	...	6 40	9 25	....
6½	Church Road	...	8 43	10 5		....	1213	1 23	3 5	....	....	5 8	....	...	6 45	9 30	....
7½	Machen 109	...	8 48	1010		....	1218	1 28	3 10	....	....	5 12	....	...	6 50	9 36	....
—	Trethomas	...	8 52	1014		....	1222	1 32	....	....	....	5 16		...	6 55	9s41	
10¼	Bedwas	...	8 56	1018		....	1226	1 36	3 20	....	....	5 20		...	6 59	9 45	
15¼	Maesycwmmer and Hengoed	...	9 6	1028		11 20	1235	1 46	3 30	4 35	....	5 30	Saturdays only.	...	7 9	9 55	Saturdays only.
17	Pengam & Fleur-de-lis .. arr.	...	9 11	1033		11 25	1240	1 51	3 35	4 40	....	5 35		...	7 14	10 0	
—	Pengam & Fleur-de-lis dep.	...	9 25	1037		....	1243	1 56	....	4 41	....	5 38		...	7 25	10 5	
17¾	Bargoed and Aberbargoed	...	9 29	1042		....	1248	2 2	....	4 45	....	5 43		...	7 30	10 10	
18¾	Cwmsyfiog and Brithdir ..	...	9 33	1046		....	1252	2 6	....	4 49	....	5 47		...	7 33	10s14	
19½	New Tredegar and Tirphil.	...	9 37	1051		....	1257	2 12	....	4 53	....	5 52		...	7 37	10 20	
21	Abertysswg .. Pontlottyn 111	...	9 42	1056		....	1 2	2 17	....	4 58	....	5 57		...	7 42	10 26	
22	Rhymney and Pont- arr.	...	9 45	11 1		...	1 5	2 20	....	5 1	....	6 0		...	7 45	10 29	
—	Pengam & Fleur-de-lis .. dep.	...	9 16	Stop		11 30	Stop	Stop	3 40	Except Saturdays.	....	....	5 40	...	7 20	....	....
18¾	Bargoed Junction 111	...	9 27			11 41			3 47		4 45	....	5 45	...	7 29	....	1010
20¾	Darran and Deri	...	9 34	....		11 48	....	....	3 54		4 53	....	5 51	...	7 39	....	1017
23½	Fochriw	...	9 43	....		11 57	....	....	4 4		5 1	....	5 59	...	7 51	....	1025
26½	Dowlais Top ‡	...	9 50	....		12 4	....	....	4 12		5A8	....	6 6	...	8 1	....	1032
28	Pant .... arr.	...	9 54	....		12 8	aft	aft	4 16		5A12	....	6 10	...	8 6	....	1036
—	Pant .... dep.	850	10 0	....		12A10	1 14	3 40	4 20		....	....	6 14	7 5	8 15	....	1041
28¾	Pantysgallog	853	10 3	....		12A13	1 17	3 43	4 23		....	....	6 17	7 8	8 18	....	1044
29¼	Dowlais § 473 .... arr.	855	10 5	aft		12A15	1 19	3 45	4 25		....	....	6 19	7 10	8 20	....	1046
28	Pant .... dep.	...	9 57	1 56		12 9	Stop	....	4 19	....	5A13	....	....	...	8 10	....	....
29½	Pontsticill Junc. *(above)* arr.	...	10 0	1 59		12 12	aft	....	4 22	....	5A16	....	....	...	8 14	....	....
—	Mls Merthyr .... dep.	...	9 35	From Dowlais at 11A59 mrn., *see above.*	1155	12 10	2 45	....	4 0	....	....	....	....	...	7 50	....	....
—	2¾ Cefn Coed	...	9 45		12 5	12 20	2 55	....	4 10	....	....	....	....	...	8 0	....	....
—	4¼ Pontsarn, for Vaynor ..	...	9 50		....	12 25	3 0	....	4 15	....	....	....	....	...	8 5	....	....
—	6¾ Pontsticill J. *(above)* arr.	...	9 55		1214	12 30	3 6	....	4 21	....	....	....	....	...	8 10	....	....
—	Pontsticill Junction .... dep.	...	10 5		1216	12 38	....	....	4 28	....	....	....	....	...	8 23	....	....
31¼	Dolygaer	...	10 9		Mons. & Sats.	12 42	....	....	4 32	....	....	....	....	...	b	....	....
32¾	Torpantau	...	10 14			12 47	....	....	4 37	....	....	....	....	...	8 33	....	....
—	Pentir Rhiw	...	10V23			....	....	....	4s45	....	....	....	....	...	a	....	....
40	Talybont-on-Usk	...	10 32			1 5	....	....	4 55	....	....	....	....	...	8 53	....	....
42¼	Talyllyn Junction 582, 689 arr.	...	10 40			1 14	....	....	5 5	....	....	....	....	...	9 2	....	....
	Talyllyn Junction 582, 689 dep.	...	10 50			1 30	....	....	5 20	....	....	....	....	...	9 5	....	....
47	Brecon 689 .... arr.	...	11 0			1 40	....	....	5 30	....	....	....	....	...	9 15	....	....

NOTES.

A Mondays and Saturdays.

a Stops to set down on notice being given to the Station Master at Pontsticill or Torpantau.

b Stops to set down on notice being given to the Station Master at Pontsticill.

s Saturdays only.

t Fridays only.

u Runs on first and third Tuesday.

V Fridays; also on the first and third Tuesday in each month.

* New Tredegar and Tirphil.

† Pengam & Fleur-de-lis.

‡ About ¼ mile to Dowlais (Cae Harris) Station, G.W. & Rhymney.

§ Over ¼ mile to Dowlais (Cae Harris) Station, G.W. & Rhymney.

‖ ¼ mile to G. W. Station.

☞ For other Trains

BETWEEN — PAGE
Brecon and Talyllyn Junction.... 582, 689
Pontsarn and Merthyr 473
Bargoed and Maesycwmmer and Hengoed 111
Bassaleg and Newport 93

Bradshaw's passenger timetable for July 1922.

Maesycwmmer in connection with the Brecon service. Between the guards working the Rhymney trains and those on the Brecon service a friendly rivalry existed; the former often prevailed upon their drivers to spend the waiting time at Rhymney in remarshalling the train sets, if they had got out of order, into the most symmetrical sequence they could get of types and classes of vehicles. (One worthy even painted 'lace curtains' on the windows of his guard's van.)

There was rivalry on the footplate, too. Legends still linger of old-time drivers like Will Thomas, of the Rhymney Railway, and Clements of the B&M, who in the 1880s would lie in wait on their respective sides of the valley at Bargoed to pace one another side-by-side nearly to Bedwas, where the two railways diverged; the last 4¾ miles from Maesycwmmer to Bedwas afforded the longest station-to-station run on the Old Rumney.

Colliers' trains were an important feature of B&M operation. In the early days there were dozens of small collieries spread around the southern lines, but as time went on only the larger ones survived. The acceptance that colliers should ride to work rather than walk came soon after the turn of the century, leading to considerable purchases of old carriages by the collieries and railways. Fortunately this coincided with decisions by various urban lines to electrify, and cheap steam carriage stock was available from the Mersey, Metropolitan and North London railways. The full details of what trains were run, how much colliery stock appeared on the 'main lines', and to what extent miners' trains entered colliery lines will never be known. The B&M announced that miners' platforms had been erected at McLaren's No. 1 (at Abertysswg), New Tredegar Colliery, Elliot Pit, Coedymoeth (Cwmsyfiog) and Aberbargoed Junction, all on the Rhymney branch. Apart from the last, the job of keeping the platform lit (for much of the year needed both morning and evening) was taken on by the colliery, and they may have also paid for the platform. A halt was also mentioned as 'Opposite Llanbradach' near Bedwas.

The McLaren's trains (later Tredegar Coal & Iron Co.) worked between Maesycwmmer and McLaren No. 1 (New Tredegar), two in the early morning and one in the afternoon. When not being used, the train stood at Fleur-de-Lis sidings. Another train was contracted with Powell Duffryn. This ran from Machen also up the Rhymney branch, but of course not calling at the New Tredegar Co. halts, to Coedymoeth and Elliot Pit platforms, also calling at all stations except Fleur-de-Lis. The empty stock was stabled at New Tredegar Colliery.

A constant problem for the B&M and other railways with colliers' trains was the need to prevent the passengers 'bailing out' where it was most convenient. With such short signal sections and many coal trains to operate, stops or slow running occurred as a matter of course, and if near home, why not drop off? The miners did not buy tickets, but were issued with brass checks; the Rule Book called for railway employees to report cases of people leaving moving trains by quoting the number of the person's check, but it is very unlikely that this was carried out.

In 1922 a bus service was put on to carry miners from Rhymney to the McLarens' pits; it only lasted 18 months but by 1930 buses were making inroads into the railway workmens' traffic.

NEWPORT, NEW TREDEGAR, and BRECON.

Up. — Week Days only.

High Street,	mrn	mrn	mrn	mrn	mrn	mrn	mrn	mrn	aft	aft	aft	aft	aft	aft	aft	aft		aft	aft	aft	aft	aft	aft
Newport..........dep.		6 25		8 3			1058	1 5		2 50	340	350		450		6 45			9 5			1042
Bassaleg A............		6 37		8 12			11 9	1 14		2 59	348	359		459		6 53			9 14			1050
Rhiwderin............				8 16			1113	1 18		3 3	4 3	5 3		5 3		6 58			9 18			1055
Church Road.........				8 21			1118	1 23		3 8	4 8	5 8		7 3				9 23				11 0
Machen 82, 85......	512	6 55		8 26			1123	1 28		3 13	413	513	5 7	8		9 28						11 5
Trethomas............	520			8 33			1130	1 35		w 3 20	419	520	7 15		9 35						1112
Bedwas...............	524			8 38			1135	1 38		3103	23	422	523	7 18		9 39					1115
Maesycwmmer B....	536			8 48	9 0		1143	1 48		321	3 33	432	533	7 28	740	9 49		1020	1125
Fleur-de-lis Platform	539			8 52	9 3		1147	1 52		326	337	440	537	7 32	739	9 54		1023	1128
Pengam (Mon.)......	542		W	8 55	9 6		1149	1 54	W	326	3 39	440	541	7 34	746	9 59		1026	1134
Pengam (Mon.)...dep.	543	634		753		9 7			1 55	220	327		441		542	6 40			747	10 0	1020
Aberbargoed.........	550	641		810		913			2 4		335		446		548	6 45			753	10 8	
Cwmsyfiog...........	556	647		8 5		918			2 10	232	339		451		553	6 51			755	1014	1032
New Tredegar..arr.	6 0	651		8 9		921			2 14	236	343		454		556	6 54			8 1	1019	1036
Pengam (Mon.)...dep.				8 56			1150	Stop		3 40			441		Stp	7 35				1027	1135
Bargoed 88				9 5		1110		1159		3 48			447 aft			7 43	825			1035	1141
Darran and Deri ¶..				9 11		1116		1213		3 54			4 9		511	7 49	831			1041
Fochriw...............				9 26		1131		1219		4 9			5 2		512	8 4	845			1056
Dowlais Top..........				9 35		1140		1228		4 18			511		516	8 13				11 5
Pant 91 ....arr.				9 39		1144		1233		4 22						8 18				11 9
Dowlais (Central) ſarr.				10 0				1 29		4 35						8 26				1120
91 ⎩dep.				9 33				1220		4 5						8 0				
Pant..............dep.				9 42		1145		1235		4 25			517			8 20				
Pontsticill Junction arr.				9 46		1149		1239		4 29			521			8 24				
Merthyr N 96.{ſarr.				1024				1 30 aft		6A19					619	8 51				
⎩dep.				9 28			1130	1210	1246		4 0						7 55			
Pontsticill Junction dep.				9 51			1157	1243	1 13		4 33						8 28			
Dolygaer.............				9 55				1247	K		4 37						8 32			
Torpantau...........				10 2				1252			4 43						8 38			
Pentir Rhiw.........				1010				1 1			4 51						8 46			
Talybont-on-Usk....				1018			1229	1 9	1 34		4 59						8 54			
Talyllyn Junc. ¶ ſarr.				1026				1 17			5 7						9 2			
150, 699 ⎩dep.				1032				1 30			5 19						9 4			
Brecon 89, 699.....arr.				1041				1 38			5 23						9 12			

Down. — Week Days only.

...¶ ....dep.	mrn	mrn	mrn	mrn	mrn	mrn	aft	aft	aft	aft	aft	aft	aft	aft	aft	aft	aft	aft	aft	aft	aft
...¶ ....dep.			745				12 5		2 0	Z	w 450		610					
...lyn Junction ſarr. ⎩dep.			754				1214		2 9		459		619					
...bont-on-Usk......			756				1218		216		5 8		621					
...ir Rhiw............			8 1				1223		221		513		530	627				
...antau..............			815				1237		235		527			640				
...gaer...........[96			830				1251		250		541			655				
...sticill Junction arr.			835				1258		254		546			659				
			839				1 2		258		550			6 67		3		
...rthyr N 96..{ſarr.			9 9				1 30		337	519	619		629	734				
⎩dep.			810				1210		238	525			633					
...sticill Junction dep.			844				1 5		321	Stp	Stp		7 7					
91 ....arr.			847				1 9		3 4		528		711					
...wlais (Central) ſ arr.			9 0				1 29		321		531		Stp		722			9 22	9 29
91 ⎩dep.			835				1220		243						655			9 33
...ais Top			848			1240	1 12		3 5		532		712				9 38
...riw ¶..............			859		1248	1 17		310		5 25	537		717				9 45
...an and Deri ¶...			824	9 9		1257	1 26		318		5 32	544		724	853			9 54
...ed 88			829	917		1 5	1 35		326		5 41	553		733	8 1			10 0
...am (Mon.)/above/arr.				921			1 42		335		5 48	6 0		740	9 7			10 4
...am (Mon.)/above/arr.							1 48		339 aft		aft		aft	744			10 5
New Tredegar..dep.	6 2	620	725	830		11 0		1 25		142	238		355		610	710			9 25		9 50	1039
Cwmsyfiog...........	6 8	626	728	833		11 3		1 28		148	243		358	5 5		613	713			9 28		9 54	1044
Aberbargoed [(above)	614	631	733	838		11 8		1 33		154	248		4 2	510		618	718			9 33		10 1	1049
Pengam (Mon.) arr.	620	637	737	842		1112		1 37		159	254		4 7	513		622	722			9 37		10 7	1054
...am (Mon.)....dep.		638	738	843		920	1113		1 38	147	2 0	255		340	4 8		514		723	745		9 38	10 6		1055
...de-lis Platform...		641	741	846		926	1116		1 42	150	2 5	258		343	411		517		726	748		9 41	10 9		1058
...cwmmer B........		644	747	850		930	1120		1 46	152	2 8	3 2		347	415		521		729	752		9 45	1012		11 2
...as................			758			940	1130		1 52		2 20	312		356	425		531			8 2		9 55			1112
...omas.............			8 1			943	1133				2 8	315		359	428		534			8 5		9 53			1115
...en 82............			8 7			949	1139				2 13	320		Aa						810		10 3			1120
...ch Road..........			812			954	1144				2 18			Aa 441	529	543					815		10 8		
...derin............			817			959	1149				2 23			410	437	548					820		1013		
...leg A...[125, 699			822			1021	152				2 27			4 0	447	450	558	552				824		1017		
...port G.64,69,80.arr.			830			1012	1 1				2 35			410	427	458	546	6 1				832		1025		

About ¼ mile to Bassaleg Junction Station   A Arr 5 19 aft on Sats commencing 16th inst.   Aa Stops when required
About ¼ mile to Hengoed Sta   E Except Sats   G High St   H Thro Carrs (one class only) Treherbert (dep 11 12 mrn) to
...erystwyth, via Builth Wells, pages 84 and 150   K Thro Train (one class only) Barry to Llandrindod Wells
3 14 aft), via Builth Wells. pages 84 and 150   L Sats only, commences 16th inst
r N One class only   S or S Sats. only   W Workmen's Train, 3rd class only
Thro Train (one class only), Llandrindod Wells (dep ¢ 19 aft) to Barry, via, Builth Wells, pages 150, and 84

Thro Carrs (one class only) Aberystwyth (dep 12 5 aft) to Treherbert (arr 7 55 aft) via Builth Wells pages 150 and 84
"Halts" at Ogilvie Village between Darran & Deri & Fochriw, & at Groesffordd, between Talyllyn Junction & Brecon.
OTHER TRAINS between Newport and Bassaleg, page 81—Newport and Merthyr, page 85—
Talyllyn Junction and Brecon, pages 150 and 699.

The Merthyr to Talyllyn pick-up goods working running on to the east loop at Talyllyn East junction on 28th July, 1951. *T.B. Sands*

A view of faithful No. 17 shunting at Merthyr in 1922. *L.C.G.B., Ken Nunn Collection*

Chapter Ten
Goods Traffic

The cleavage between the 'Brecon' and 'Rumney' sections of the B&M was even more marked in the working of the goods traffic. In the south, the Rhymney Valley coal trains were the best revenue-earners the company had, because the relatively easy grades of the Old Rumney enabled them to be worked very economically; indeed, for many years the formality of goods brake-vans was dispensed with on this section (as it was at one time on the Taff Vale), and old-timers told of portentous caravans of from 80 to 120 loaded coal wagons gently pushing a single engine down to Bassaleg. By contrast, the Brecon section freight trains, although much less heavily loaded, were almost invariably double-headed, with frequently a third engine in rear, over the terrific banks between Talyllyn and Merthyr.

The method of working on this northern section was to marshal the traffic at Talyllyn, where a considerable exchange business was done with the Cambrian and Midland Railways, and where the B&M had established an engine-shed about 1869; local trips were run between Talyllyn and Brecon. Traffic moved in full train-loads between Talyllyn and Pontsticill or Merthyr; Pontsticill – a busy place half a century ago – was the exchange point for traffic to and from Dowlais, Pantywaen, and (usually by not more than one train a day) Bassaleg. At Merthyr the B&M goods trains served both the Great Western and the Taff Vale depots.

With the acquisition of the Hereford, Hay & Brecon route by the Midland Railway, there was a considerable growth of traffic between the Midland system and South Wales by this route while by 1913 – the peak year of the South Wales coal trade – the Brecon & Merthyr was carrying nearly 3½ million tons of coal, and 277,000 tons of other minerals. So long as coal remained the supreme fuel for marine purposes, there was an appreciable amount of special train working to the Cambrian line with bunker or export coal for Birkenhead.

North of Oswestry this was now able to travel by way of the Cambrian branch from Ellesmere to Wrexham and the Wrexham Mold & Connah's Quay Railway to join the Great Central at the River Dee, a final flowering of the old dream of the all-Welsh railway from south to north. This was a pretty desperate route for goods trains, with fierce gradients, and weight restrictions, mostly single track, but by 1918 the appetite of the Grand Fleet at Scapa Flow for Welsh coal had jammed all other possible routes, and the so-called 'Jellicoe Specials' (named after the Admiral of the Fleet) began to roll from the mines via the B&M and the Mid-Wales section of the Cambrian to Oswestry and the North.

The southern part of the line, being in an area of great industrial growth for the first 30 years, benefited from events, such as the sinking of a big new coal mine at Pengam in 1906. In the same year a connection was made off the line near Barry Junction to a quarry at Trehir, and 150,000 tons of stone moved down the line for use in the Newport Docks extension. By the same token, as the depression hit after World War I, and the coal strikes brought collieries to a standstill, the railway's goods revenue suffered heavily. Finally, after World War II the coal mines and steelworks began one by one to reach the end of their life, and under British Railways the heavy side of the goods traffic ran down.

Empty wagons formed an important part of the traffic. One colliery manager stated that the supply of wagons was every bit as important as raising coal. The Company had to know how many empties the various sidings would take, and how many were already there – how this was done before the days of the telephone is hard to imagine. The Cyfarthfa collieries had a 'common user' policy; any of their wagons could be returned to any colliery; it is probable that Powell Duffryn did the same. But there were also small pits whose wagons had to be sorted out or sought for anywhere between Cardiff and the Mersey.

The B&M did not have exclusive access to any large colliery or ironworks complex, but such companies adopted a policy of using various railways and ports so as to be able to switch quickly if one became congested. Also, much of the B&M was 'through route'. Before 1914 its own returns showed that half the tonnage of goods carried on the line was in trains of other railways. This would include general goods on Cambrian and Midland trains between Brecon and Talyllyn, but most would be accounted for by coal trains of the Barry or Rhymney using its lines. For example in 1906 three-quarters of a million tons of coal from the Pontypridd area went via Penrhos and Energlyn Junctions at Caerphilly and over the B&M through Machen and Bassaleg.

At the northern end the local traffic in livestock, animal feed, manure, lime and timber remained fairly steady until in the mid-thirties these commodities began to move by road. General merchandise also, after the railways were no longer in competition, tended to go by less arduous railway routes; although the usefulness of the main line for south-to-north traffic remained, it was not enough to ward off complete closure; for the northern half of the B&M the twilight world of 'goods only' suffered by many lines lasted only a few years.

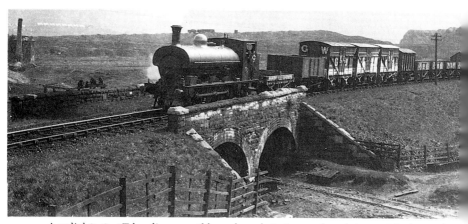

A radial 0–6–2T heading a northbound goods train seen here between Merthyr and Cefn. Note the quarry plateway passing beneath the bridge.   *Ken Nunn Collection*

Chapter Eleven
Accidents

Many railways in their early years had 'run-away' accidents, and with its gradients the B&M was not likely to be an exception. The first was quite minor. On 14th November, 1867, when the branch to Merthyr was still only open as far as Cefn, the early afternoon train to Brecon was nearing Torpantau on the 1 in 47 grade when a rake of wagons carrying rails, which had been shunted at the station, ran away and met it a mile south. However, visibility was good and the driver had time to get his train into reverse. The second accident at Talybont on 8th June, 1868, was more serious. A goods train of 18 vehicles with engines and brake vans both front and rear, was edging its way down the 'Seven Mile Bank' going north. It should have kept to a speed of about 12 mph but about half-way down it began to gather way; the drivers and guards took what action they could, but brake-blocks were soon burning, so much so that the smoke obscured the view from the rear of the train. So far, not a disaster; but at Talybont the staff were messing about with some ballast wagons which had arrived earlier from Talyllyn and were trying to shoulder them over the station crossover when the run-away bore down on them. The result was a pile of debris and stone dust and one driver dead. Three railway servants were indicted for manslaughter, but the cases were not brought to Court.

On 14th February, 1874 a passenger train was derailed near Brithdir on the Rhymney branch; one passenger was killed and five injured.

'Wild runs' continued as long as wooden brake-blocks did – incidentally, the B&M preferred poplar wood. A bad one occurred on 2nd December, 1878 when a goods train of 36 wagons, with *Hercules* and *Atlas* on the front and *Severn* behind, got out of control on the 'Seven Mile Bank' and was totally wrecked when it derailed, killing four enginemen. It was bitterly cold and the train crew were very tired; the guard – who admitted that he did not stop at the east end of the tunnel to pin down brakes, as he should have done – worked from 5 am to 8 pm one day and 4 am–12.10 pm the next, for 22s. a week. The brakesman had been on duty for 13 hours 10 mins, and the fireman of *Hercules* – the only survivor of the four men on the leading engines – had begun work at 3 am; it was then nearly 9.30 pm! So away went the train down the 1 in 38 to its doom; the brake-power of three engines and the van was quickly overborne; the drivers reversed their engines without avail, pieces of disintegrated motion being later found on the track two miles from the bottom of the bank. Here the speed was estimated at 60 miles an hour, and ¼ mile south of Talybont station, after the abutments of two bridges had been struck either by part of the train or by flying pieces of engine-motion (the connecting-rod of *Hercules* was found near the canal bridge), the train went off the road and over a 16 ft embankment, at a point where there was a curve of 22 chains radius, which was considered safe for 40 mph. All the enginemen were killed with the exception of the fireman of *Hercules* and the driver of *Severn*.

Some remarkable evidence about the working on 'Seven Mile Bank' in those primitive days was given at the Board of Trade inquiry. 'Wild runs' were clearly of frequent occurrence; the driver of *Severn* said he had been concerned in three, and the Talybont ganger testified to having seen trains

A print showing the effect of the runaway accident of 16th May, 1874 when a rake of wagons broke loose forcing a train and locomotive into the end wall of Merthyr High Street station, damaging the Brunel wooden roof as well. *Author's Collection*

2−4−0T No. 12 derailed between Pontsticill Junction and Pant; the date is uncertain. This engine was built in 1889 by R. Stephenson to works No. 2659 and finally withdrawn in February 1923. The GWR No. 1452 was allocated but never carried by the locomotive. *Author's Collection*

run wild through the station 'scores of times'. The management were already sufficiently cautious to have stipulated a form of double-block working, whereby no train was allowed to leave Torpantau for Talybont if there was already a train on the road between Talyllyn and Talybont, and vice versa. The Inspecting Officer, Colonel Rich, expressed the view that block telegraph working alone was not safe, and that staff-and-ticket should be introduced (as it duly was), also that train loads on the bank should not exceed 10 wagons per engine, and that the loads of two or three engines should not be made up into one train.

The danger from minor 'runs' where speed did not go high enough to derail was reduced by progressively extending the Talybont loop across the river and up the Llansantffraid cutting, thus allowing the counter gradient to bring the train under control.

Accidents of a similar nature also occurred in the south. The earliest recorded accident was a collision on Graigyrhacca Curve, between Machen and Bedwas, in September 1864, during the period when the Old Rumney was in process of conversion from a tramroad to a railway proper; a descending loaded coal train collided with an ascending train of empties (both trains being worked by locomotives), and 26 colliers who were riding to work on the empty wagons were injured.

Another accident took place on the Rumney section on 10th June, 1868, when the six-coupled goods engine *Antelope*, which was hauling an up goods train on trials after being overhauled in Machen shops, became derailed on a curve of less than six chains radius, just after passing under the Newport, Abergavenny & Hereford viaduct at Maesycwmmer. The engine, tender, and part of the train went off a bridge into the road beneath, killing both the driver and John Kendall, locomotive superintendent of the Rhymney Railway, who was present at the trial by invitation of J.T. Simpson, the Brecon & Merthyr's first locomotive superintendent. Simpson himself, a Glaswegian aged 42, died four days later from his injuries; his grave in Machen churchyard is marked by a headstone which was erected by public subscription.

More serious was the accident in Merthyr (High Street) station on 16th May, 1874, when a B&M passenger train which had just arrived at the platform was run into by 21 goods wagons which had broken loose from a Vale of Neath mineral train and had run back down the bank from Merthyr Tunnel. The B&M train was virtually wrecked and the engine (again *Antelope*) forced through the buffer-stops and nearly into the street; there were some 50 casualties, one of which proved fatal.

Chapter Twelve
Locomotives (to 1923)

The bipartite early development of the B&M was strongly reflected in the locomotive history of the line. For some years at the outset the management was uncertain where to locate the headquarters of this department; the Northern Section was served by a running-shed, with limited repair facilities, at Brecon (Watton), but there was a rival establishment, primarily for repair purposes, at Machen on the Old Rumney. Colloquially known as 'The Foundry', this may well have been inherited from the Rumney Railway, which had authorised the hire or purchase of locomotives as early as 1856, and which also gave hospitality to those belonging to freighters who hauled their own traffic over the tramroad. After the union of the two sections of the B&M in 1868, the management toyed with the idea of building new works either at Brecon or within the triangle of lines at Talyllyn, but Machen finally won the day on the score of its greater handiness to sources of coal and materials and of the preponderance of motive power at the southern end of the line. Until about 1908, when a diversion was carried out, the main line ran through the works area, as at Crewe and Wolverton.

Successors to the ill-fated J.T. Simpson as locomotive superintendents of the B&M were Thomas Mason (from 1869), Charles Long (1873), G.C. Owen (1888), and James Dunbar (1909). Like Simpson, Owen lost his life in tragic circumstances on his own railway, being run over by a train near his official residence at Machen. The last holder of the title of locomotive superintendent was Mr Dunbar; after his death on 26th February, 1922, H.F.H. Gibson, 'held the fort' until the GWR took over on 1st July of the same year.

Locomotive practice followed the usual pattern of the bigger South Wales railways in beginning with a fair proportion of tender engines, but turning over to tank engines exclusively because of their better adhesion and brake-power on the steep gradients and their versatility for either train-working or shunting in colliery sidings. After 1868, most of the tender engines were drafted to the easier grades of the Rumney Section and the heavier duties were entrusted to the six-coupled saddle tanks, which were the predominant type until the advent of Dunbar's modern 0–6–2Ts. The last tender engine was gone by 1890.

The history of the early locomotives reveals many doubts and discrepancies even in the company's own records, due mainly to the arrangement whereby the B&M and several neighbouring lines were worked under contract by Savin & Ward, who moved engines about between one system and another to meet the emergencies of the moment and without much regard to the actual ownership of the locomotives. Moreover, the B&M had no numbering system of its own until about 1880, identifying the early engines solely by names, which – further to confound the research worker – were liable to be changed for no very evident reason.

Nomenclature owed allegiance to various sources; thus *Brecknock*, *Beacon*, and *De Winton* (after the first B&M Chairman) betoken local associations; *Lady Cornelia*, *Blanche*, and *Sir Ivor* suggest tactful subservience to the Guest dynasty of Dowlais – although this was not always successful, as Sir Ivor Guest vigorously opposed some of the Brecon & Merthyr's extension projects. *Wynnstay* and *Glansevern* were names of

This Sharp, Stewart engine, built in 1865, worked briefly on the Cambrian Railway as Savin's No. 48 before transfer to the B&M as No. 9, and named *Usk*. It was renumbered 21 in 1888, the last tender engine to run on the B&M, was converted to a tank engine in 1895, and scrapped in 1904.   *Locomotive Publishing Co.*

One of the two Sharp, Stewart & Co. 0−6−0STs ordered in 1880, No. 17 seen here at Merthyr. Built in 1881 to works No. 2975, No. 17 had a new boiler in 1902 and was used mainly on the Merthyr and Dowlais branches for goods traffic. These were the oldest engines absorbed by the GWR, this one renumbered 2190 and finally withdrawn in May 1934.   *L.C.G.B., Ken Nunn Collection*

One of the two 0−4−2s, *Wynnstay* No. 12 built in October 1859 (makers' No. 1146, Sharp, Stewart) which were subject to a legal argument with the Cambrian and purchased by the B&M in August 1867. Sold in May 1884 to J. Bright. This engine was usually shedded at Newport.   *Oakwood Collection*

A Sharp, Stewart 0−6−0 tank No. 27, *Hercules* built in June 1871 (works No. 2166) and sold in February 1899 to the Bute Works. These tanks differed from the previous batch by having a larger tank capacity of 900 gallons.   *Locomotive Publishing Co.*

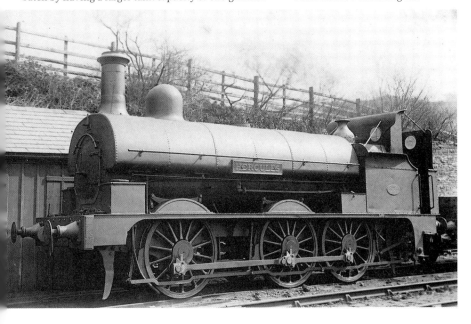

Cambrian Railways origin, transferred with the engines, while the significance of *Allt* and *Tor*, which came from the Neath & Brecon, is elusive: *Allt* is Welsh for 'a wooded hill', but *Tor* sounds more Devonian than Welsh, unless it was a corruption of *Tawe*. Whatever the reason, it proved too much for the gentleman who was by then responsible for naming the engines, and after *Allt* and *Tor* the company stuck to numbers only.

The late adoption of a numbering system for B&M engines, and the extensive switching about between Savin and the companies, makes the locomotive register rather disjointed (*see page 80*); it has necessarily been compiled in sequence of inclusion in B&M stock rather than of construction. Moreover, there were a few engines which belonged to the Brecon & Merthyr or were lent, hired, or merely appropriated for short periods, of which so little is known that they have had to be omitted; the principal omissions are *Fairy*, *Dart*, *Leon*, and *Stag*, which figure in an official list of engines dated 1865 and were all sold or broken up by 1870.

An example of the confusion is the 0–6–0 *de Winton* which some writers have shown as Cambrian Railways No. 16. It is more likely that it was No. 16 in Savin's list, and was used in the north for some purpose after the first four of the B&M's own engines arrived; in any case, it came back to the B&M later, and was numbered 6.

From contemporary press reports it is possible to prove that the first locomotives to work the line were *Pioneer* (later *Blanche*), *Usk* and *de Winton*. The first-named was a light saddle-tank of a well-known Manning, Wardle design (their No. 35, 1861); the second was a similar engine, known later as '*Little Usk*' as there was a tender engine of the same name; this was Manning, Wardle 58. The third one mentioned was a 0–6–0 tender engine, Manning, Wardle 41 of 1862. A fourth engine mentioned early was another Manning, Wardle 0–6–0ST, No. 49 of 1862, first called *Hereford* but from 1869 *Lady Cornelia*. This had been ordered by Savin on behalf of the HH&BR.

It is known also that the B&M made use of four 0–4–2 engines built by Sharp, Stewart in 1859 for Savin's railways to the north; two of them, *Glansevern* and *Wynnstay* were to remain on the line as detailed below. What seems to have happened is that after the opening runs from Brecon, Savin sent the light saddle tanks away for contracting work, and brought down from Llanidloes and points north enough goods and passenger engines, regardless of nominal ownership, to equip the Brecon shed to work the Hereford and Dowlais services. However, he also ordered engines which would be the beginning of the proper B&M engine series (though numbers were not carried at that time): Sharp, Stewart 0–6–0s *Alexandra* (later 1), and *Brecknock* (No. 2), both built 1863; also two 0–6–0ST engines, *Pandora* and *Jupiter*, Sharp, Stewart 1863, later Nos. 13 and 14. For the Rumney end, two 0–6–0 engines *Caerleon* and *Caerphilly*, Sharp, Stewart 1865, were ordered by the Rumney Company. Both these later became saddle-tanks, Nos. 4 and 5.

After the Savin crash, both the Brecon & Merthyr and the Cambrian were busy trying to trace missing engines, which both companies claimed as their property, but which were sometimes found in unexpected quarters. Thus,

John Fowler & Co. of Leeds supplied six of this class of 0–6–0ST, of which No. 3 was one. Built January 1886 to works No. 5054 and numbered 2179 by the GWR it was finally withdrawn in October 1926. This engine was equipped with steam brakes and had a new boiler in 1911. The GWR fitted its own smokebox and chimney after grouping.

Lens of Sutton

Leon and *Dart* were run to earth at Ynyslas, at the mouth of the River Dovey, having been carried off by Savin for construction work on the Aberystwyth & Welsh Coast Railway. *Pioneer* and *(Little) Usk*, which the B&M suspected the Cambrian of harbouring, actually turned up on another Savin contract, the Caernarvonshire Railway; but the star example was surely that of the little 0–4–0ST *Mountaineer*; this had been loaned by Savin to the B&M, and when the Cambrian demanded her back as being its property, discovered the B&M had hired out the engine to the Dowlais Iron Company!

In 1863 a Joint Committee of the railways which would shortly join up as the Cambrian Railways purchased most of Savin's engines and carriages, and thereafter leased them to him to operate the lines. In 1867 the Cambrian Railways claimed a sum of over £16,000 for the hire of engines to Savin, the bulk of it (£12,102) being in respect of engines used to work the Brecon & Merthyr.

These and other similar disputes caused much bad feeling and acrimonious correspondence between the Brecon and Cambrian companies and brought them to the verge of costly litigation, but, oddly enough, the most widely published incident of the tangled situation is almost wholly apocryphal. The story goes that when the B&M became disamalgamated from the Hereford, Hay & Brecon in 1868, some of the latter's locomotives, including the two 2–4–0 tender engines *Usk* and *Wye*, were seized by the B&M in lieu of unpaid debts. What actually happened was that *Usk* and *Wye* were delivered to the Cambrian in April 1865, but by October of that year had been transferred to the B&M, being replaced by two similar engines *Gladstone* and *Palmerston*, which Savin had intended for working the HH&B. (It needed something much faster than either the Brecon & Merthyr or the Cambrian to keep up with Mr Savin!) After the Savin crash, the Cambrian demanded the return not only of *Usk* and *Wye*, but also of four Sharp 0–4–2s Savin had 'lent' to the B&M. The latter tried to retain all eight engines, but after some sharp legal exchanges had to be content with *Usk* and *Wye* (later Nos. 9 and 10), and with being allowed to buy the 0–4–2s *Glansevern* and *Wynnstay* (later Nos. 11 and 12), the rest being surrendered.

Two actually acquired were 0–6–0 tender engines built by Slaughter, Gruning & Co. in 1857 and 1858; they were named *Antelope* and *Elephant* and numbered 7 and 8 on the B&M. The origin of these engines is obscure, but they had undoubtedly seen previous service. It seems probable that they may have been Cambrian Railways Nos. 32 and 33, which are stated to have been goods engines transferred to the B&M but there are not sufficient particulars available to identify them with certainty. They were long-boiler engines and had outside frames and inside cylinders. The latter were 16 in. by 24 in., and the wheels were 4 ft 6½ in. in diameter. The weight distribution was: leading 8 tons 4 cwt., driving 10 tons 15 cwt., trailing 10 tons 19 cwt., total 29 tons 18 cwt. The tenders were on six 3 ft 6 in. wheels with a base of 10 ft 7 in., and carried 1,350 gallons of water and 35 cwt. of coal.

At a meeting in 1870 the Chairman reported that the company now had 23 locomotives. Those not previously mentioned were *Vulcan* (No. 3) a Sharp Stewart 0–6–0 which had been Cambrian No. 20, and Nos. 18–23, a series of long-boiler 0–6–0ST engines named *Atlas*, *Beacon*, *Cyclops*, *Cymbeline*,

Locomotive *Usk* (later called '*Little*' *Usk*) was one of Savin's Manning, Wardle engines (built December 1862, works No. 58) seen here at Talybont on construction work in 1868; it was later B&M No. 15 but it was withdrawn in 1871 and finally sold in July 1881 to C.D. Phillips. *R.W. Kidner Collection*

Another of the Sharp, Stewart 0–6–0STs, *Cyfarthfa*, No. 24 built in August 1870 to works No. 2059 and withdrawn in 1896. The locomotive was sold in March 1897 to Crawshay Bros of Cyfarthfa Ironworks. *Locomotive Publishing Co.*

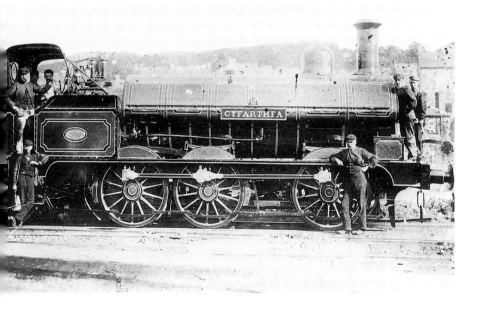

0–6–0ST No. 8, built in March 1884 by R. Stephenson, and seen here in GWR days as No. 2184. Finally withdrawn in July 1933. It is interesting to note that No. 8 retained its polished brass work up to 1915. *Lens of Sutton*

Formerly No. 42 ordered in 1913 from R. Stephenson & Co. seen here in GWR days as No. 1084. Withdrawn from use in November 1947. *Locomotive Publishing Co.*

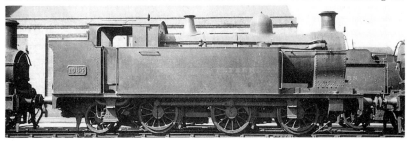

This is the sister engine to No. 17 (*see page 64*) but this time as GWR No. 2191. Originally built 1881 to works No. 2974 by Sharp, Stewart & Co. and numbered 11 (later in 1889 renumbered No. 18) *see page 76*. No. 2191 was allocated to Newport Division until scrapped in April 1932, withdrawn in May 1934 and put up for sale, finally cut up in February 1935 with a total mileage of 1,107,330. *Lens of Sutton*

No. 43 was a further locomotive built by R. Stephenson in May 1914 (works No. 3580). She became GWR No. 1113 but re-numbered in October 1947 to 428 and finally withdrawn in August 1950 after seeing service at Port Talbot.

Late D.S.M. Barrie Collection

This Fowler (built August 1885 to works No. 4995) is 0−6−0ST No. 1. It carried the GWR No. 2177 after the grouping and was scrapped in February 1928.

L.C.G.B., Ken Nunn Collection

This engine, No. 39, was one of a series of fifteen modern styled tanks built by R. Stephenson (works No. 3382 in 1910). This locomotive was taken over by the GWR and numbered 504, being scrapped in 1948.   *Late D.S.M. Barrie Collection*

In November 1906 the B&M bought two 0–6–0STs built in 1886 at Swindon (1661 class) from the Bute Works Supply Co. This locomotive shown was No. 34 (works No. 1087) and GWR No. 1694 after grouping, finally withdrawn in December 1926 as a pannier tank.   *L.C.G.B., Ken Nunn Collection*

Severn and *Mersey*. These were excellent machines with 4 ft 6 in. wheels, 17 in. × 24 in. cylinders, and a 12 ft 2 in. wheelbase. With 750 gallons of water and 18 cwt. of coal they weighed 35½ tons, 13¾ of which fell on the rear axle; what the B&M needed for its many steep banks. They were built by Sharp, Stewart from 1865 to 1868.

On the other hand the three Manning, Wardle saddle tanks were not a lot of use. The had 3 ft 1 in. wheels, cylinders 12 in. × 17 in., and a 10 ft 9 in. wheelbase; the saddle tank carried 450 gallons, and the total weight was 16½ tons, far too light for braking a train on a bank. In fact they were all later sold. *Hereford* seems to have travelled much; it was in the Cambrian shops at Oswestry in 1868, and must then have gone south, for in the same year it was renamed *Lady Cornelia*. This lady, one of the Churchill family, of Duke of Marlborough fame, married in that year Sir Ivor Guest, the Dowlais ironfounder. If compliment was intended, it somewhat misfired, for two years later we find the engine working as a pumping engine at Brecon!

The B&M was not primarily a passenger line, but found good use for the two 2–4–0 engines it inherited from Savin's stock, *Usk* and *Wye* – the former not to be confused with *Little Usk* which was one of the three Manning, Wardles. With 5 ft 6 in. driving wheels they were fast, and 16 in. × 20 in. cylinders gave them enough power; both were built by Sharp, Stewart in 1865 and served on the Cambrian before the Savin sort-out. Somewhat older were the two ex-Cambrian 0–4–2 engines, *Wynnstay* and *Glansevern* – both names inappropriate on their new line. With 5 ft coupled wheels and 15 in. × 22 in. cylinders, they were built by Sharp, Stewart in 1859 and made good enough mixed traffic engines.

Another batch of six Sharp, Stewart long-boiler 0–6–0STs now appeared. Nos. 24–9, differing only from the earlier ones in larger saddle tanks and 5 inches more wheelbase; their names were *Cyfarthfa, Sir Ivor, Samson, Hercules, Rumney* and *Taff*. All were sold on at the end of the century to various works.

The next two acquisitions were due to the decision by the Neath & Brecon Railway to hand over the working of their line from Brecon to the Midland Railway. This reduced their need for engines, and two Avonside 0–6–0ST engines, *Allt* and *Tor* were sold to the B&M, becoming Nos. 30/1. They were double-framed engines, built in 1865, differing from the Sharp, Stewarts in having larger bunkers carrying two tons of coal. They worked very satisfactorily and were not withdrawn until 1921. In fact they long outlived their fellows, for all other original engines had been sold or scrapped by 1905.

It was policy to keep the number of engines to 30, this being sufficient for the traffic in a fairly stable period after the big expansions. New engines took over old numbers, and the first two replacements were Nos. 11 and 17, more Sharp, Stewart 0–6–0ST engines but not of the long-boiler type, the firebox being in front of the rear axle rather than behind it.

Having had good service from its two ex-Neath & Brecon engines, the Company now ordered 12 more outside-framed 0–6–0STs: Nos. 6, 7, 8, 5, 15, 16 from R. Stephenson & Co. and Nos. 1, 2, 3, 4, 13, 14 from J. Fowler & Co. The two batches were built in 1884 and 1885 respectively.

The B&M had by now consciously eschewed tender engines, partly because with so many water points tenders were not required, and also because a tank engine was handier for the mixed kind of duties required. There was as yet however no real passenger tank engine, and casting around for a suitable design, the company borrowed a GWR 2−4−0T, with outside frames to the leading axle and inside main frames. It was satisfactory, and a series of six imitation engines was obtained from Stephensons from 1888 to 1904 (Nos. 9, 10, 11, 12, 25, 21). They became the standard engine on the Brecon to Newport run, and when clean their smooth tank sides showed up the red livery to better advantage than did the saddle tanks.

Replacement mineral engines were also required, and four of these were of the 0−6−2ST type, rare on British railways; they had 4 ft 7½ in. driving wheels and radial trailing wheels of 3 ft 6 in. They were numbered 23, 24, 19 and 20, built from 1894 to 1905. Meanwhile two more outside-framed 0−6−0STs had been bought, Nos. 22, 24, this time built by Kitsons; and Nos. 23 and 26 from Vulcan Foundry. Finally three more, Nos. 27−9 were ordered from Nasmyth Wilson in 1900.

After 1900 for a few years capital was short and recourse had to be made to second-hand engines to meet what was now an increasing traffic demand. In 1906 two 0−6−0ST engines were bought from the GWR, Nos. B&M 33/4; they had been built at Swindon in 1887, and with 5 ft 1 in. wheels and weight overall of nearly 48 tons they outclassed the earlier engines. One more (No. 32) was purchased next year. An odd item was an outside-framed 4−4−0PT bought from the Ebbw Vale Steel & Iron Co, in 1908; the latter had bought it shortly before from the Bute Works Supply Co., who had it from the GWR, the builders, in 1898. It was their first 'pannier tank' and unusually had wooden Mansell wheels on the bogie. It seemed to please nobody and was sold to its fifth owner, the Cramlington Coal Co. in 1916.

By 1909 with easier capital and a new locomotive superintendent, James Dunbar, more new engines were ordered: a series of eight inside-framed 0−6−2Ts built by Stephensons from 1909 to 1914 (Nos. 36−43). They had 18½ in. × 26 in. cylinders, 4 ft 6 in. coupled wheels, increased boiler pressure (175 lb.); of the total weight of 67 tons, 54 tons 6 cwt. was available for adhesion. Three tons of coal and 1740 gallons of water were carried. The specification called for the ability to work the equivalent of 10½ loaded 10 ton wagons plus brake van up a gradient of 1 in 40. They were ideally suited to the mineral traffic, though also fitted with the vacuum brake for working passenger trains. Three more (45−7) were purchased in 1915, and Nos. 48−50 in 1921.

To the last, the Brecon & Merthyr could not resist a bargain and the ex-LSWR Adams 4−4−2T (B&M 44) built as a 4−4−0T in 1879 was acquired in 1914, and an ex-ROD dock tank bought through Government disposals six year later. The Adams tank proved insufficiently powerful for the main line passenger service and was swiftly relegated to the 'Second Division', the Rhymney branch, where she worked in odd partnership with No. 35, the 4−4−0 pannier tank, until the latter was sold.

The colour scheme of B&M locomotives was brick-red, with panelling by a broad black band lined each side with thin yellow lines; the buffer beams were painted vermilion lined black, with yellow numerals shaded black. During World War I goods engines passing through Machen shops were

No. 23, 0−6−2ST built at Vulcan Foundry in May 1894 to works No. 1405, allocated GWR No. 1692 and finally withdrawn in July 1925 and cut up at Stoke-on-Trent. Rarely seen at the Southern end of the line, mainly used around Merthyr. No. 23 was rostered on a Royal Train in June 1896.   *I.H. Smart Collection*

Stephenson 0−6−0ST No. 7 of 1884, seen here as GWR 2183. She was scrapped in 1932.   *L.C.G.B., Ken Nunn Collection*

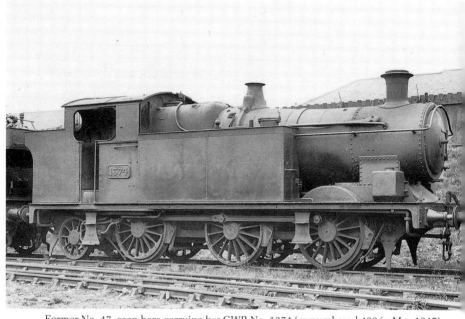

Former No. 47, seen here carrying her GWR No. 1374 (re-numbered 433 in May 1947). The locomotive was built by R. Stephenson in 1915 (works No. 3647) and finally scrapped in 1951. *W.L. Good*

This is 0–6–0ST No. 18 in her original shape as built in 1881 by Sharp, Stewart to works No. 2974 (previously No. 11). *L.C.G.B., Ken Nunn Collection*

One of five 0−6−0 of a class built by Kitson and Nasmyth. This locomotive No. 28 was built by Nasmyth (works No. 585) in September 1900 and became GWR No. 2172 at the grouping being finally withdrawn in May 1928. This particular locomotive was fitted for burning patent fuel during the coal strike of 1921.

Locomotive Publishing Co.

A class of six 'Metro styled' 2−4−0T were ordered between 1888 and 1904. This engine, No. 25, was the last but one to be built (1898 to works No. 2878) and allocated GWR No. 1458 (but never carried) being scrapped in October 1922.

L.C.G.B., Ken Nunn Collection

turned out in unlined black, except that Nos. 17 and 18 retained their brick-red livery. Exceptions to the general colour scheme were No. 44, the ex-LSWR 4−4−2T, which was painted a dark crimson lake, and the final series of 0−6−2Ts (Nos. 45−50) and the ex-ROD tank No. 35, which were nearer red-brown than brick-red.

There were five engine-sheds on the system, the number of locomotives stationed at each in 1922 being shown in brackets: Bassaleg (28), Rhymney (2), Dowlais (2), Talyllyn (1), and Brecon (14). There had however earlier been engine sheds at Talybont (closed early), and at Fleur-de-Lis and Pont-sticill, which were closed during World War I. At Brecon the Midland shared the B&M shed, while the Cambrian had a separate one nearby. For many years the water supply at Brecon had to be pumped from the canal, hence the frequent references in the records to old engines being used as stationary pumpers. Talyllyn shed was closed almost immediately after absorption of the line by the GWR; Bassaleg continued in use until 1929, when the engines were transferred to the Newport depots, and Rhymney shed went out of existence after the closure of the Rhymney branch north of New Tredegar, to be described later. Dowlais Central shed was closed on 8th May, 1960. Machen shops were closed in 1927 and their work transferred to the enlarged Caerphilly Works nearby.

The B&M drivers regarded their engines very much as individuals. Driver John Drayton sent this note to the author some 40 years ago.

> Engines of the B&M Nos. 1, 2 and 3 'Dolls' ended their days on the pilots; Nos. 2 and 3 on the High Street Goods Yard Pilot, they were saddle tanks with steam brake exhaust through the cab roof (1926). They were left-handed engines, (L.H. crank leading going forward) and springing between leading and driving axleboxes compensated. No. 1668 (B&M No. 49) was altered from L.H. to R.H. crank leading by the GWR, without success inasmuch as they were always kept on the Ebbw Pilot jobs. They seldom wandered from the shadow of the Transporter Bridge.

> The B&M had no shunters. Guards marshalled trains, sometimes under the guidance from 'Controllers' (there were only two) who hung out in a cabin on the end of Bassaleg station. Drivers acted upon their own judgement in the way of locomotive management. Johnny Clements carried a gadget on his engine to unite two broken sections of valve spindles which oftimes gave trouble. Locomotive Inspectors were not carried on the paysheets. Enginemen were practical operators and performed wonders with their little engines which they worshipped.

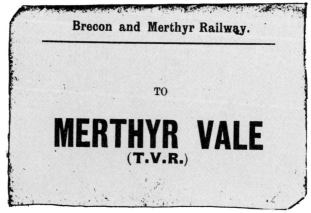

Luggage label showing Merthyr Vale which was a Taff Vale Railway station.

A good side view of B&M 2−4−0T No. 11 built in 1889 by R. Stephenson, later to become GWR No. 1460.   *R.C. Riley Collection*

A view of No. 21, the last of the 2−4−0Ts in the class of 6 to be built in 1904 by R. Stephenson.   *R.C. Riley Collection*

Table 1

LOCOMOTIVES OF THE BRECON & MERTHYR RAILWAY

No. and Name	Wheel Arrangement	Year Built	Builders	Works No.	GWR No.	Year Withdrawn	Remarks
1 Alexandra	0–6–0	1863	Sharp, Stewart	1408	—	1885	Sold for scrap, June 1885
2 Brecknock	0–6–0	1863	Sharp, Stewart	1409	—	1884	Sold to Rhymney Iron Co.
14 Jupiter	0–6–0ST	1863	Sharp, Stewart	1471	—	1886	
13 Pandora	0–6–0ST	1863	Sharp, Stewart	1472	—	1885	
4 Caerleon	0–6–0	1865	Sharp, Stewart	1587	—	1886	Nos. 4 and 5 to order of Rumney Railway
5 Caerphilly	0–6–0	1865	Sharp, Stewart	1588	—	1889	No. 5 lent to Rudry Co., 1889; sold for scrap, 1890
18 Atlas	0–6–0ST	1865	Sharp, Stewart	1657	—	1888	Sold to Rhymney Iron Co.
19 Beacon	0–6–0ST	1865	Sharp, Stewart	1658	—	1905	Used as stationary pumping engine, Brecon, until 1908, when sold
20 Cyclops	0–6–0ST	1866	Sharp, Stewart	1665	—	1905	Sold through P. Stevenson, Liverpool, to Garswood Hall Colliery, Wigan
21 Cymbeline	0–6–0ST	1866	Sharp, Stewart	1666	—	1889	To Bute Works Supply Co.
22 Severn	0–6–0ST	1868	Sharp, Stewart	1853	—	1896	
23 Mersey	0–6–0ST	1868	Sharp, Stewart	1854	—	1891	–
7 Antelope	0–6–0	1857	Slaughter, Gruning	–	—	1881	–
8 Elephant	0–6–0	1858	Slaughter, Gruning	–	—	1882	–
10 Wye	2–4–0	1865	Sharp, Stewart	1579	—	1887	ex CR 47
9 Usk	2–4–0	1865	Sharp, Stewart	1580	—	1904	ex CR 48. R/N 21 in 1888; reb. as side-tank. 1895
3 Vulcan	0–6–0	1862	Sharp, Stewart	1342	—	1886	ex CR 20
6 De Winton	0–6–0	1862	Manning, Wardle	41	—	1882	ex CR 4
12 Wynnstay	0–4–2	1859	Sharp, Stewart	1146	—	1884	ex CR 6
11 Glansevern	0–4–2	1859	Sharp, Stewart	1148	—	1881	
16 Lady Cornelia	0–6–0ST	1862	Manning, Wardle	49	—	1871	Formerly Hereford; renamed by CR when repaired at Oswestry, 1869. From 1871 stationary pumping engine at Brecon: sold 1882 to Tuthill Limestone Co.
15 ('Little') Usk	0–6–0ST	1862	Manning, Wardle	58	—	1881	Sold to C.D. Phillips, 1881
17 Blanche	0–6–0ST	1861	Manning, Wardle	35	—	1880	Originally Savin's No. 10 Pioneer; renamed c.1871; sold to Rhymney

No. and Name		Wheel Arrangement	Year Built	Builders	Works No.	GWR No.	Year Withdrawn	Remarks
25	Sir Ivor	0–6–0ST	1870	Sharp, Stewart	2087	—	1897	Sold to Rhymney Iron Co.
26	Samson	0–6–0ST	1871	Sharp, Stewart	2144	—	1893	Sold to Bute Works Supply Co., 1900
27	Hercules	0–6–0ST	1871	Sharp, Stewart	2166	—	1899	Sold to Bute Works Supply Co., 1900
28	Rumney	0–6–0ST	1872	Sharp, Stewart	2261	—	1900	Sold for scrap 1902
29	Taff	0–6–0ST	1872	Sharp, Stewart	2260	—	1899	Sold to Bute Works Supply Co., thence Consett Iron Co.
30	Allt	0–6–0ST	1874	Avonside	1013	—	1921	DF ex N&B, Ncs. 7 and 8. Purchased 1877
31	Tor	0–6–0ST	1874	Avonside	1014	—	1921	
11		0–6–0ST	1881	Sharp, Stewart	2974	2191	1932	R/N 18, 1889
17		0–6–0ST	1881	Sharp, Stewart	2975	2190	1934	—
6		0–6–0ST	1884	R. Stephenson	2447	2182	1927	DF
7		0–6–0ST	1884	R. Stephenson	2448	2183	1932	DF
8		0–6–0ST	1884	R. Stephenson	2497	2184	1933	DF
5		0–6–0ST	1884	R. Stephenson	2498	2181	1927	DF
15		0–6–0ST	1884	R. Stephenson	2499	2187	1923	DF
16		0–6–0ST	1884	R. Stephenson	2500	2188	1928	DF
1		0–6–0ST	1885	J. Fowler	4995	2177	1928	DF
2		0–6–0ST	1885	J. Fowler	4996	2178	1925	DF
3		0–6–0ST	1886	J. Fowler	5054	2179	1926	DF
4		0–6–0ST	1886	J. Fowler	5055	2180	1926	DF
13		0–6–0ST	1886	J. Fowler	5056	2185	1923	DF
14		0–6–0ST	1886	J. Fowler	5057	2186	1934	DF
9		2–4–0T	1888	R. Stephenson	2656	1402	1923	—
10		2–4–0T	1888	R. Stephenson	2657	1412	1923	—
11		2–4–0T	1889	R. Stephenson	2658	1460	1924	—
12		2–4–0T	1889	R. Stephenson	2659	1452	1923	—
25		2–4–0T	1898	R. Stephenson	2878	1458	1922	—
21		2–4–0T	1904	R. Stephenson	3121	—	1921	—
23		0–6–2ST	1894	Vulcan Foundry	1405	1692	1925	—
26		0–6–2ST	1894	Vulcan Foundry	1406	1833	1924	—
22		0–6–0ST	1896	Kitson	3668	2169	1927	DF
24		0–6–0ST	1896	Kitson	3667	2170	1928	DF
27		0–6–0ST	1900	Nasmyth, Wilson	584	2171	1932	DF
28		0–6–0ST	1900	Nasmyth, Wilson	585	2172	1928	DF
29		0–6–0ST	1900	Nasmyth, Wilson	586	2173	1932	DF
19		0–6–2ST	1905	Vulcan Foundry	2040	1674	1923	—

LOCOMOTIVES OF THE BRECON & MERTHYR RAILWAY

No. and Name	Wheel Arrangement	Year Built	Builders	Works No.	GWR No.	Year Withdrawn	Remarks
20	0-6-2ST	1905	Vulcan Foundry	2041	1677	1928	—
33	0-6-0ST	1887	GWR, Swindon	1086	1693	1931	Purchased 1906 ⎫ Previous GWR Nos. resumed in 1922
34	0-6-0ST	1887	GWR, Swindon	1087	1694	1926	Purchased 1906
32	0-6-0ST	1886	GWR, Swindon	1078	1685	1934	Purchased 1907 ⎭
35	4-4-0PT	1898	GWR, Swindon	1702	—	1916	DF ex GWR 1490. Purchased 1908 from Ebbw Vale Co. Sold March, 1916, to Cramlington Coal Co.
36	0-6-2T	1909	R. Stephenson	3379	11	1949	—
37	0-6-2T	1909	R. Stephenson	3380	21	1950	R/N 422, 1947
38	0-6-2T	1909	R. Stephenson	3381	332	1949	—
39	0-6-2T	1909	R. Stephenson	3382	504	1948	Delivered January, 1910
40	0-6-2T	1914	R. Stephenson	3577	698	1951	R/N 425, 1947
41	0-6-2T	1914	R. Stephenson	3578	888	1950	R/N 426, 1947
42	0-6-2T	1914	R. Stephenson	3579	1084	1947	—
43	0-6-2T	1914	R. Stephenson	3580	1113	1950	R/N 428, 1947
44	4-4-2T	1879	Beyer, Peacock	1840	1391	1922	B. as 4-4-0T for LSWR (No. 376). Reb. as 4-4-2T. Nine Elms, 1883. Purchased (as LSWR 0376) by B&M 1914. OC.
35	0-6-0T	1917	Kerr, Stuart	3070	2161	1929	R.O.D. No. 605. Purchased 1920. Sold May 1929, to Ashington Coal Co. OC.
45	0-6-2T	1915	R. Stephenson	3645	1372	1953	R/N 431, 1949
46	0-6-2T	1915	R. Stephenson	3646	1373	1953	R/N 432, 1948
47	0-6-2T	1915	R. Stephenson	3647	1374	1951	R/N 433, 1947
48	0-6-2T	1920	R. Stephenson	3798	1375	1953	R/N 434, 1949 ⎫ b. 1920 but delivered February, 1921
49	0-6-2T	1920	R. Stephenson	3799	1668	1954	R/N 435, 1950
50	0-6-2T	1920	R. Stephenson	3800	1670	1954	R/N 436, 1949 ⎭

(Locomotives still in service at 1st January, 1948, retained their GWR numbers as BR numbers.)

Abbreviations:

CR   Cambrian Railways   PT   Pannier Tank
DF   Double Frames   Reb.   Rebuilt

Table 2

LEADING DIMENSIONS

The following are the dimensions of coupled wheels and cylinders respectively, generally in the order of the preceding list:

Engine Nos.	Coupled Wheels	Cylinders (in.)	Weight (tons)
1, 2	5 ft 0 in.	$16\frac{1}{2} \times 24$	–
14, 13	3 ft 9 in.	$16\frac{1}{2} \times 22$	$26\frac{3}{4}$
4, 5, 3	4 ft 6 in.	16×24	26
18–29	4 ft 6 in.	17×24	$35\frac{1}{2}$
7, 8	4 ft 6½ in.	16×24	$29\frac{3}{4}$
10, 9	5 ft 0 in.	16×20	$24\frac{3}{4}$
6	4 ft 6 in.	16×22	–
12, 11	5 ft 0 in.	$15\frac{1}{2} \times 22$	–
16, 15, 17	3 ft 1 in.	12×17	$16\frac{1}{2}$
30, 31	4 ft 0 in.	17×24	–
11, 17 (of 1881)	4 ft 6 in.	17×24	38
1–8, 13–16 (1884–86)	4 ft 2 in.	17×24	45
9–12, 25, 21 (2–4–0Ts)	5 ft 1 in.	16×24	43
19, 20, 22–24, 26–29 (1894–1905)	4 ft 7½ in.	17×26	$49\frac{1}{4}$
32–34 (ex GWR)	5 ft 1 in.	17×26	–
35 (4–4–0PT)	4 ft 7 in.	$15\frac{1}{2} \times 26$	–
35 (ex ROD)	4 ft 0 in.	17×24	$48\frac{3}{4}$
36–43	4 ft 6 in.	$18\frac{1}{2} \times 26$	67
44 (ex LSWR)	5 ft 7 in.	18×24	59
45–50	5 ft 0 in.	18×26	61

Nos. 17, 18, 22–9, 32–4 rebuilt as pannier tanks and weight differed slightly.

Nos. 36–43 rebuilt with GWR boilers, weight 62½ tons.

Nos. 45–50 rebuilt with GWR boilers, weight 59¼ tons.

LOADS OF ENGINES IN DRY WEATHER.

The following tabular statement shows the Load of each class of Engine up the gradients named in dry weather, but in wet or slippery weather, the Loads must be proportionately less :—

ENGINE Nos.	Bassaleg to Machen	Machen to Fleur-de-lis	Fleur-de-lis to Rhymney	Fleur-de-lis to Bargoed R.R.	Bargoed R.R. to Deri	Deri to Pantywaen	Pontsticill to Torpantau	Torpantau to Talybont	Talybont to Talyllyn	Brecon to Talyllyn	Talybont to Torpantau	Pontsticill to Pantywaen	Machen to Caerphilly	Caerphilly to Machen	Dowlais Branch	Merthyr to Pontsticill
2, 3, 4, 5, 6, 7, 8, 14, 15, 16, 22, 24, 28, 29, 32, 33,	24	33	25	25	15	12	15	15	13	24	11	19	22	45	24	14
18, 19, 20, 23, 30, 31	22	31	23	23	13	10	13	13	12	22	10	17	21	38	22	13
37, 38, 39	32	44	33	33	20	16	20	20	17	32	15	25	29	60	32	19
Ruling Gradient	1 in 82	1 in 234	1 in 96	1 in 94	1 in 47	1 in 38	1 in 47	1 in 38	1 in 40	1 in 76	1 in 38	1 in 50	1 in 59	1 in 200	1 in 40	1 in 45

Ordinary Wagons to count as 7 Tons Loaded.
5 Assorted Goods to count as 4 Loaded.
5 Medium Empties to count as 2 Loaded.

2 Ten Ton Wagons to count as 3 Loaded.
2 Ten Ton Empties to count as 1 Loaded.
3 Small Empties to count as 1 Loaded.

LOADING OF DOWN MINERAL TRAINS.

Rhymney to Fleur-de-lis	Guard only	50 loaded wagons	Fochriw Pits to Deri Junc.	Guard only		20 loaded wagons
do.	Guard & Brakesman	65 ,,	do.	Guard & Brakesman	30	,,
Fleur-de-lis to Bassaleg	Guard only	65 ,,	Deri Junction to Aberbar-			
do.	Guard & Brakesman	85 ,,	goed Junction	Maximum Load	50	,,

This Load List is exclusive of the Guard's Van, which is taken as attached to each train.

NOTE.—Nos. 9, 10, 11, 12, 21, 25 and 35 are Passenger Engines; maximum load—8 four-wheeled Vehicles between Bargoed R.R. and Talyllyn.

Dated July 1909

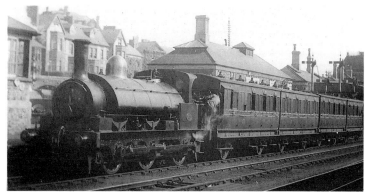

A train of ex-Mersey Railway stock stands at Newport High Street station, date unknown.   *HMRS Society*

Brecon & Merthyr Railway full brake (short) No. 37, after withdrawal by the GWR in 1922.   *British Railways*

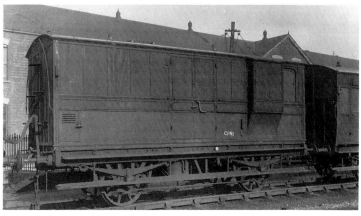

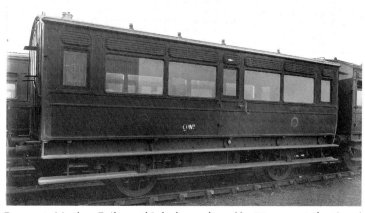

A Brecon & Merthyr Railway third class saloon No. 57, seen at the time it was condemned by the GWR in 1924 (GWR re-numbered the coach No. 9180, but it was never carried).   *Courtesy late D.S.M. Barrie Collection*

Chapter Thirteen
Carriages

The earliest carriages were built by Adams of Birmingham and started arriving in 1862. It is not known what livery was adopted, but from a local press report describing them as 'glaring' it may have been red. They would have been of the same type as supplied to other 'Savin' lines: four-compartment Seconds and 1st/2nd Compos and five-compartment Thirds. The latter were very primitive, with no compartment divisions above seat level, and lit only by two oil lamps in the roof for all five compartments. The Annual Report for 1870 lists the carriage stock as: two second class, eighteen Thirds, eleven 1st/2nd Compos, two 2nd/3rd Compos, and four guards vans. These last were of considerable importance, bearing in mind the working of the seven-mile bank, though their weight was probably only ten tons; guards were trained to make successive brake applications to avoid flat wheel rims, but there must have been times when the brake was screwed down and left down.

None of these carriages survived to be taken over by the Great Western, so little is known of them in detail. Nor is it known whether the HH&B had any carriages of its own. When open only to Hay it was worked by the Newport Abergavenny & Hereford Railway and its successors (in rapid order) the West Midland Railway and the GWR. After Savin's crash it was worked by the Cambrian and then the Midland, so if it had any passenger stock it would have gone in with that of the B&M during the 'amalgamation'.

The B&M began purchasing carriages from the Metropolitan Carriage & Wagon Co. in 1877 or earlier, including a batch of 22 ft 1st/2nd compos and 25 ft Thirds. By the turn of the century 26 ft 8 in. was the normal length. When the carriage stock was renumbered, Nos. 1–57 were all of MCW build, Thirds and 1st/2nd Compos, except for two brake Thirds (16, 28), two saloon (20, 57), a carriage truck (42), a horse-box (43) and five full brakes (36–8, 48/9). At some time also No. 28 was replaced by one of three ex-Mersey Railway carriages bought at third-hand from the Manchester & Milford Railway in 1906. Nos. 58–63 were Mersey carriages bought direct in 1903, No. 64 an inspection saloon from Ashbury's.

We now enter the period when the B&M could not afford new carriages, and as its requirements for miners' transport were rising, resort was had to second-hand stock. Nos. 65–7 came from the Metropolitan Railway in London after it electrified, and Nos. 68/9 were two more Manchester & Milford 'Merseys'. Nos. 70–100 came from the London & South Western Railway in 1910–15 and were all six-wheeled except for two brake Thirds; also the series was broken by Nos. 87/8 which were ex-Metropolitan Railway horse-boxes. No less than eight of the LSWR stock were full brakes.

After the War the company turned to a dealer in Trentham to purchase Midland Railway second-hand carriages, three four-wheeled full brakes (101–3), Compos Nos. 104–6 and Thirds Nos. 107–114. The Midland vehicles were six-wheeled (apart from the brakes) being 30½ ft long, against the 33 ft 11 in. of the longest LSWR six-wheelers.

At Grouping it was clear that the B&M stock was inferior to that of most other lines taken over, and most was scrapped at once, though a few carriages had further life as service vehicles, and Compo. No.14 was sold to the Bishop's Castle Railway. The last ex-B&M carriage to run seems to have been No. 52, scrapped in 1971 after 30 years in capital stock and 47 further years as a mess van.

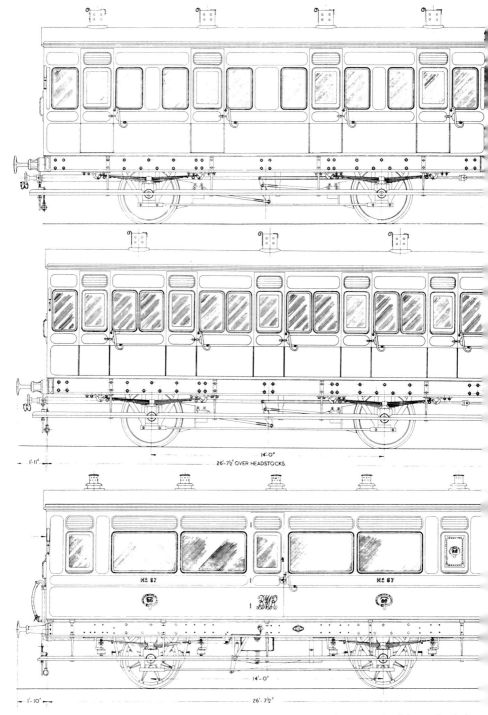

14'-0"

26'-7½" OVER HEADSTOCKS.

1'-11"

N° 57   N° 57

B¤R

14'-0"

26'-7½"

1'-10"

A Brecon & Merthyr standard First four-wheeled coach (*top*), Third four-wheeled
coach (*centre*) and Third Saloon coach (*bottom*). There were two saloons, Nos. 20 and
57. Both were built between 1893 and 1894 and withdrawn at the grouping or just
after.   *Drawings by courtesy of The Model Railway Constructor*

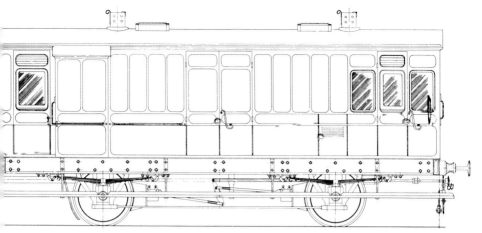

Only one of these Brecon & Merthyr brake thirds was ever built (1899), numbered 39 and later to become GWR No. 4327.

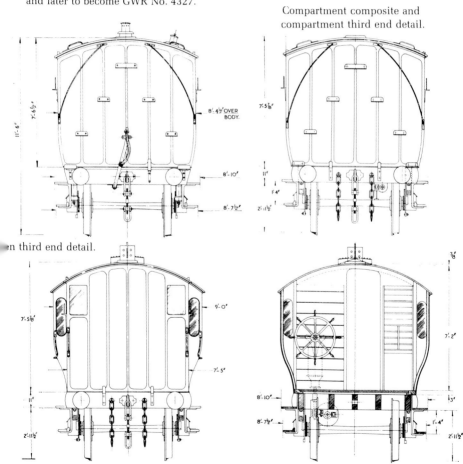

Compartment composite and compartment third end detail.

...en third end detail.

...ake third and full brake end detail.

Cross section of brake third and full brake.

Fourteen 4-wheelers from the 'eighties which had been classed by the B&M as workmens' carriages were given GWR Nos. 4321-34 but remained in B&M livery, though it is doubtful whether this was discernible under the grime.

The only available carriage list is that prepared at Grouping, and this cannot be entirely relied upon. For instance, in 1909 the B&M reported they had replaced an old 2nd/3rd Compo. with a new Third, but none built in that year appears in the list; the report added that there were 69 passenger vehicles.

The two saloon carriages, Nos. 20 and 57, built respectively in 1893 and 1894, apparently carried the full livery, with BMR monogram on the door (which was in the centre) and garter emblems at both ends of the side panels, the numbers being in gold shaded red; the garter was also engraved on the windows of the end lavatory. They were described as painted dark purple, though the normal colour is given as chocolate or sometimes dark red. The dignity of these saloons was somewhat diminished by the use of spoked wheels instead of the more usual hardwood-cored Mansell wheels, as had most of the stock which was not second-hand. The B&M catered for all three classes throughout its life, as second class was not abolished until 1st July, 1923.

It is of interest that where the railway's armorial device was used, there was an error in the rendering of the Brecknock shield, with three bats being shown as three bees!

'Foreign' stock was of course seen regularly on B&M lines, especially the PC&N section, and on the through trains from Newport to Aberystwyth, on which Cambrian Railway stock was used, including some relatively sumptuous bogie stock.

To what extent colliery-owned carriages appeared is not certain. Powell Duffryn are said to have had six Mersey Railway carriages, but as the B&M itself also had some of these, there might be some confusion. At the time that the Great Western took over, the carriages allotted to miners' trains by the B&M comprised five 'Merseys', one ex-Metropolitan, two ex-LSWR and six of their own old ones. Such trains sitting in White Rose siding all day, covered in coal-dust, probably did not display their ownership. A photograph of the 1928 collision at New Tredegar reveals that No. 5 of the private workmen's train was a former Midland Railway bogie coach.

The Brecon & Merthyr was relatively early in the field in adopting for its passenger trains a semi-continuous (but non-automatic) brake, this being the Fay & Newall mechanical hand-brake controlled by the guard; when the latter wound his brake-wheel, the action was transmitted to adjoining vehicles by a rotating rod. It did not normally apply to more than four or five coaches, but as any B&M train in excess of this length normally had two brake-vans and a brakesman as well as a guard, the arrangement worked. Later the company adopted the vacuum automatic brake. In other coaching matters it was less progressive; the 1905 Appendix mentions no form of heating other than foot-warmers, while steam-heating and gas-lighting did not become general until about 10 years later.

For the information of collectors of tickets, the respective colours of B&M tickets were First Class, white; Second, dark purple; and Third, green.

A double-headed through train to Aberystwyth leaving Merthyr; the carriage stock is
Cambrian-owned. *L.C.G.B., Ken Nunn Collection*

A fine view of a 2−4−0T with a Merthyr train arriving at Cefn Coed about 1920.
L.C.G.B., Ken Nunn Collection

An R.C.T.S. railtour on 22nd June, 1952 with GWR Railcar No. 24 seen here at Brecon
(Watton) old station.   *Late D.S.M. Barrie Collection*

No. 3768 arriving at Brecon with the 4.20 pm Neath Riverside service on 4th August,
1962. This short section between Free Street bridge and the station was owned by the
B&M but used exclusively by the Neath & Brecon and Midland Railways.
                                                                        E. Wilmshurst

Chapter Fourteen

Route and Stations

(Written as in the last years of running)

BRECON TO NEWPORT

The layout at Brecon (Free Street) has already been described. Leaving the station there are carriage sidings on both sides, and at Brecon Junction (Heol Lladron) the line can been seen descending to the former Watton station. There was formerly a signal box here, but from 1931 only a ground frame. After a mile of level, the line begins to rise through Groesffordd Halt (2 m.) to the tunnel, which is on a 1 in 421 up grade. Immediately at the east mouth the points divide into double line for Talyllyn station (4 m.). As this platform was used for all trains to Llanidloes (Mid-Wales) and Hereford (MR) as well as B&M ones, delay was sometimes caused in dispatching trains from Brecon when the Talyllyn platform was occupied. Therefore in 1898 an extra platform was built, east of the West signal box, on the North Loop, at which non-BMR trains could halt and thus leave the main platform clear. All three sides of the Talyllyn triangle were built for double line (or doubled soon after opening), but the only one so used was the North Loop; on the East and West Loops one line was used for running and one for shunting. Several sidings were laid in, also a B&M engine shed (in 1869) which could only be entered by using the Mid-Wales North Junction at first, though some years later a line was laid from the West Loop, to the shed, a carriage shed and some sidings. The three boxes at the junctions of the triangle were for some time known by numbers: North No. 1, West No. 2, East No. 3. Talyllyn was the station for Llangorse Lake until the GWR built a halt on the Mid-Wales line.

After half a mile of easy gradients, comes the plunge at 1 in 40 down to Talybont (6¾ m.). Here a large water tank was set beside the main building on the southbound platform, with water points on both platforms. The neat little engine shed at the south end, northbound side, remained (out of use) to the end, though the turntable which existed in front of it was replaced by a little-used siding. Approaching the station from the north the line crossed the River Usk at Llansantffraid; the double line had previously continued across this bridge (the earlier wooden version has been mentioned) and up into the cutting, to protect the southbound trains from goods trains in the opposite direction which might have overrun the station. Beyond the station the line crosses over the Brecknock & Abergavenny Canal, later referred to as the Brecon & Newport canal, and in GWR ownership. (Talybont, which sported a 6 ton crane, remained open for goods traffic up to 1st July, 1963.)

Now begins the 'Seven Mile Bank' at 1 in 38; this is broken only for a very short length of level at Pentir Rhiw station (10 m.). This has a very short platform, with a large signal box and a loop; its most important possession however is a runaway relief siding, leading off the northbound side and running for over a hundred yards on a slight curve to a dead-end in a wood; the last portion is laid on concrete pot sleepers with iron tie-bars. Marked as a halt on maps, it was not so-called by the railway. Though now apparently very remote, it served more habitations before the two mile-long reservoir beside the line was built by the Newport Waterworks in Glyn Collwyn in the

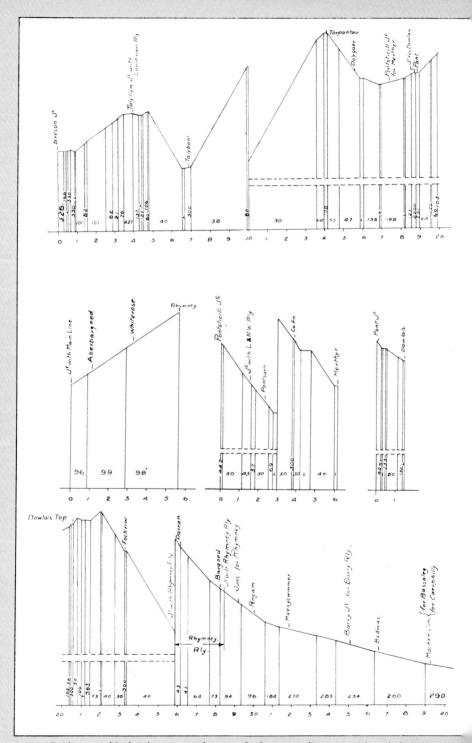

Gradient profile for the system showing the heavy gradients over the whole line.

'thirties. There was formerly a siding on the lake side of the station for Newport Corporation.

The track bed of the old Bryn Oer Tramway is running close on the east side as we pull up from Talybont canal bridge, but it is climbing more quickly, and it is 200 ft higher along Clyn Collwyn and 300 ft higher away in the woods at Pentir Rhiw. The B&M now turns west, but the old tramway continues south, dodging round the mountain to the vast Trevil Quarries. Here there was another tramway running to Rassa and Beaufort, but probably no physical connection. The Bryn Oer went on to join a tramway at Bryn Oer Patch to Rhymney Iron Works.

There is now a further 4 miles of bank, and about the middle of this the railway put in a water point for emergencies, although water was also available at Torpantau. The tunnel itself is on a severe curve and the train enters facing north-west but emerges facing south. Torpantau was not an original station, though from the first trains stopped for water and for pinning down brakes; there are two short sidings at the south end for banking engines, coming off the northbound line. Torpantau first appeared, as a conditional stop, in the 1870 tables, quoted as 13¾ miles from Brecon, but now given as 14 m. The gradient is now down at 1 in 47, and does not break for Dolygaer station (15½ m.). This is a simple platform and offers no goods facilities.

Pontsticill Junction (17¼ m.) has three platform faces, the southbound one being an island; the signal box is at the north end of the northbound one. There is a carriage siding and a small delivery siding for goods; earlier there had been a private siding for the New Tylerybont Stone Co. From Pontsticill the Merthyr branch diverges gradually to the west, and joins the ex-LNWR line from Abergavenny. At Pant (18¾ m.) there is a lower platform for trains on the short branch to Dowlais. The line now enters an area of once-great iron works, mainly cleared during the past 40 years. Rising at 1 in 60 it approaches Dowlais Top (20½ m.). Just beyond the station the ex-LNWR spur to the Abergavenny line runs off on the south, and we pass over that line. Immediately after this there was once a B&M spur on the west side to the Rhymney Limestone Railway; this originally ran from the Twynnau Gwynnion quarries, east of the joint line at Merthyr, and across the B&M main line and down to Rhymney. Less than a mile further was a junction with the Pantywaun Tramway at Pantywaun Junction. There were colliery lines around the Rhaslas Pond, and at some date a halt was put in here for miners, which much later became the public Pantywaen Halt (21¾ m.).

Descending at 1 in 40, a siding runs off on the west side to Fochriew Colliery; by a reversal from this siding a spur runs north to join the Rhymney Railway. This 1½ mile spur was opened in 1876 by the Dowlais Iron Co. but was worked jointly by the GWR and RR. The RR also, by reason of having running powers from Deri to Pantywaun, could work coal from Fochriew via the B&M. Fochriew station is at 23¼ m. The line is still descending past Ogilvie Village Halt, mainly used by miners but staffed until 1955. This is on ex-Rhymney metals, the junction (Deri Junction) being an end-on one at 24¾ m. Darran & Deri is a Rhymney Railway station (26 m.) which was opened in 1858, as was Bargoed (28¾ m.). At Bargoed South Junction we

Talyllyn station looking west on 11th April, 1959, with the West Junction box on the right; the tunnel can be seen at the platform ends. *H.B. Priestley*

Talyllyn East Junction in 1951; the line going straight ahead led to Brecon; the loop on the right was half-owned by the B&M and half by the Mid-Wales and was the route followed by 'through' south to north trains. *T.B. Sands*

Talyllyn West Junction. On the right is the extra platform added beside the north loop, the B&M line runs to the left.   *H.B. Priestley*

The remains of the Mid-Wales Railway station at Talyllyn, in October 1950, being used as a dwelling. B&M trains used this station briefly while the new joint station was being built.   *Lens of Sutton*

Talybont station from the
showing the water tank. Photog
in April 1962.   *H.B. P*

Talybont looking south, not lon;
closure in July 1962.   *H.B. P*

A double-headed southbound
Talybont in 1904, with a
0−6−0ST piloting a 2−4−0T.
          L&GRP, courtesy I.h

Pentir Rhiw station in GWR days looking south; the signal box is huge for so small a platform. The 8.03 am from Newport hauled by 0−6−0PT No. 3661 is passing 0−6−0PT No. 9776 and van on 18th April, 1962.   *H.B. Priestley*

The long refuge siding at Pentir Rhiw, available for 'runaways' from Talybont; it curved into a wood at the end.   *H.B. Priestley*

The south end of Torpantau station in July 1958 showing the short siding (originally there were two) for the banking engines. Note the single line tablet catcher alongside the signal box. *R.M. Casserley*

Dolygaer station; this was staffed until 1932. The bleak mountainous terrain is obvious in this view, looking south. *Author's Collection*

Pontsticill station looking south; the ex-GWR pannier tank No. 9631 is in the process of reversing with tanks from Merthyr on 12th July, 1962. *H.B. Priestley*

Pontsticill Junction in 1948, with a Brecon train in the main northbound platform. Note the stabled train of clerestory stock and the abundance of milk churns.
R.M. Casserley

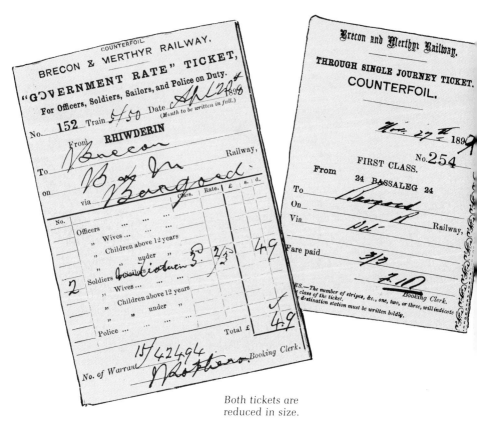

Both tickets are
reduced in size.

A view of Pontsarn for Vaynor station photographed in September 1951.   *R.W. Rush*

A train from Merthyr to Brecon awaits departure from Cefn Coed, with 0−6−0ST No. 17 at its head. Note the B&M and L&NW joint line notice alongside the water column. *L.C.G.B., Ken Nunn Collection*

A Brecon train entering a busy Cefn Coed at an unknown date, headed by an 0−6−2ST. *L.C.G.B., Ken Nunn Collection*

A local service from Brecon coming off the long, curved Cefn viaduct into Cefn Coed station, about 1920. *L.C.G.B., Ken Nunn Collection*

Vulcan Foundry 0−6−2ST No. 20 on a goods train at Cefn Coed taking on water. *L.C.G.B., Ken Nunn Collection*

0—6—0ST No. 17 on a Merthyr branch train at Morlais Junction; the tunnel for the LNWR line to Abergavenny is at the right. *L.C.G.B., Ken Nunn Collection*

The driver of a Brecon train exchanging staffs at Llwyncelyn Junction, north of Merthyr, where lines went off on both sides to join the Cyfarthfa Works railways. *L.C.G.B., Ken Nunn Collection*

A busy scene at Pant station on 24th March, 1951, looking south. The 12.40 pm Dowlais train stands in the middle headed by No. 217 whilst the 11 am to Newport (headed by No. 3770) stands at the main platform. Note the smoke venting from the LNWR line tunnel on the extreme right. *W.A. Camwell*

A platform view (c1920) of Pant main station with a train from Dowlais pulling-up from the low level platform. *J. Miller*

The lower platform at Pant, serving Dowlais Central trains, seen in 1957. The back of Pant signal box can be seen at the top of the picture. *R.M. Casserley*

Pant station from the north; a Merthyr train is leaving headed by 0−6−2T No. 45; the Dowlais branch train can be seen in the lower platform, c1922.

L.C.G.B., Ken Nunn Collection

Pant station viewed from the north in July 1958; the Dowlais branch joins beyond the left-hand platform.   R.M. Casserley

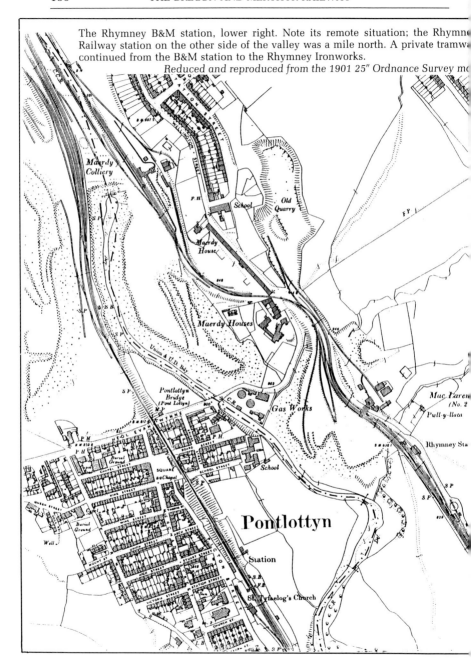

The Rhymney B&M station, lower right. Note its remote situation; the Rhymney Railway station on the other side of the valley was a mile north. A private tramway continued from the B&M station to the Rhymney Ironworks.

Reduced and reproduced from the 1901 25" Ordnance Survey map

The next three pages show station areas of some of the stations and halts on the B&M.
All courtesy of the Ordnance Survey and taken from the 25″, 1901 editions.

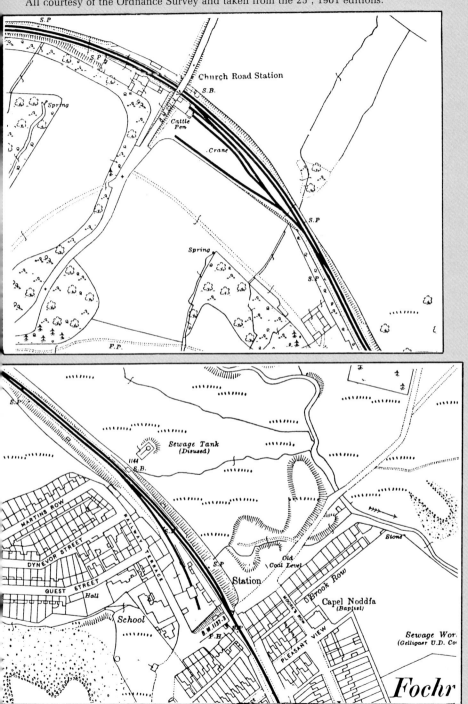

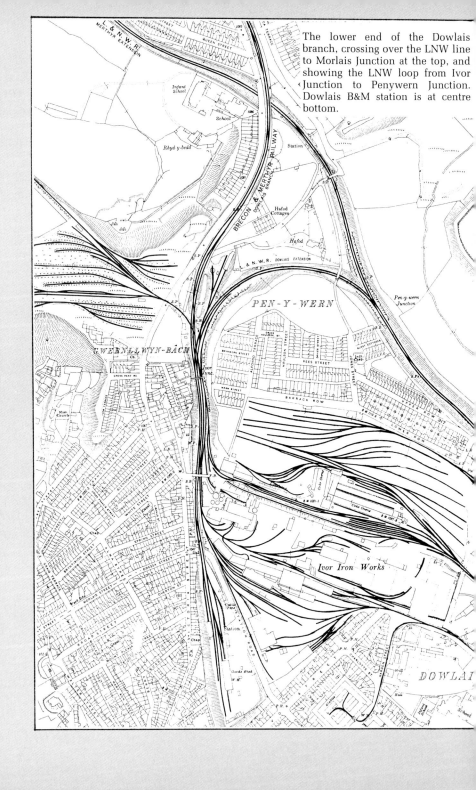

The lower end of the Dowlais branch, crossing over the LNW line to Morlais Junction at the top, and showing the LNW loop from Ivor Junction to Penywern Junction. Dowlais B&M station is at centre bottom.

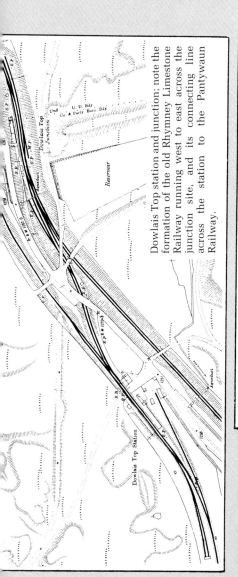

Dowlais Top station and junction; note the formation of the old Rhymney Limestone Railway running west to east across the junction site, and its connecting line across the station to the Pantywaun Railway.

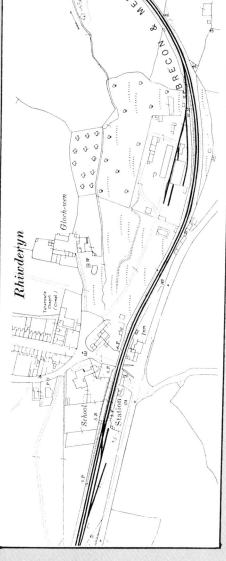

Rhirderyn

return to the B&M, and swing across the valley to meet the former B&M Rhymney Branch at Aberbargoed Junction. The Rhymney branch of the former Rhymney Railway has already diverged at Bargoed North Junction.

The next station is now called Pengam (Mon), 29¾ m., but from 1909 to 1924 was Pengam & Fleur-de-Lis, and from 1924–6 just Fleur-de-Lis, until in the latter year a halt of that name was put up (30½ m.) to bring miners closer to their work. Collieries in this area included Britannia, Pengam, Upper Pengam and Gilfach. A mile south of Pengam comes Maesycymmer Junction, where a spur line ran up.to join the GWR line from Aberdare to Pontypool, which we pass under.

Maesycwmmer (31¾ m.) was called Maesycwmmer & Hengoed from 1906 to 1924. The down grade is now quite mild; after another 3½ miles comes the site of the former junction with the Barry Railway. The magnificent Llanbradach viaduct could be seen from the line here for some years after the branch was closed, but it was knocked down in 1937. The line is now running east through Bedwas (36¼ m.), from which there were four tracks to Trethomas (37½ m.), the outer ones being relief lines for coal trains. Trethomas station was not opened until 1915; there were a number of works sidings between here and Bedwas, including the Bedwas Navigation Colliery, British Benzol, Glyn Gwyn Siding and Trehir Quarries.

At Machen (39¼ m.) the Caerphilly branch joins from the west, immediately at the west end of the platforms. Church Road (40¾ m.) was closed on 16th September, 1957; it was one of the few B&M stations advertising facilities for handling livestock. Rhiwderin (43 m.) lost its passenger service on 1st March, 1954 and goods on 14th September, 1959. Bassaleg (44 m.) is the last station on B&M metals, and is the point of junction with the private railway of Guest Keen & Nettlefold. The main locomotive running shed was located here. The tracks of the Alexandra Docks & Railway Co. run off to the south as the B&M joins the Great Western Railway 'Park Mile' through the former Tredegar Deer Park. At Park Junction the lines split, southwards to Cardiff and northwards to Newport; the centre line of the triple junction running to the docks. The southernmost tracks here are those of the ADR, which skirts Park Junction and goes to the Alexandra Docks. Newport (High Street) station is 47 miles from Brecon.

THE MERTHYR BRANCH

This branch line is a strange one in many ways; for one thing, a train which starts running south-eastwards ends up facing north-west. It also has a remarkable number of junctions, and the line falls all the way at 1 in 45 or 1 in 50. First we pass the junction with the private railway of the Vaynor Quarries to the west, one branch of which passes under the line to a works on the east side. At 1¾ m. comes the junction with the LNWR line to Abergavenny, and at 2¼ m. Pont Sarn station, which has no goods facilities and was a request stop for many years, being unstaffed from 1934 and closed on 13th November, 1961. Cefn Coed station (3¾ m.) has water points and sidings handling traffic not only from Vaynor but also from Abercryba Quarry and in later years from the Ynysfach Siding (Cyfarthfa Ironworks). The Cefn siding was connected to a mineral tramway, 4 miles in length, running up Cwm Taf and serving various lime kilns and quarries, but this was out of use before 1900. Heolgerrig Halt (4½ m.) was opened on 31st May, 1937.

As the branch enters the town itself, the site of the vast Cyfarthfa Works can be seen to the east. A private railway ran two miles southwards to the Cyfarthfa Colliery, and at Llwyncelyn Junction this was joined to the branch by a short spur on the west. Immediately a further spur of nearly half a mile ran off to the east to join the private railway from Ynysfach Works, which itself joined the Cyfarthfa railway just before the colliery. The Merthyr Branch passes under this line, but after sweeping round a curve to Rhydycar Junction, a further curve brings it to another junction with the Ynysfach railway, this portion of some ½ mile not being used by passenger trains. The main line continues to join the Great Western and so into Merthyr High Street station, which has five platforms and the remains of one of the last of the Brunel wooden roofs. Half a mile south of the station, at Mardy Junction, the GWR line joins the joint GW/Taff Vale line to Cardiff, and just south again it passes over the Taff Vale line to join the joint GW/Rhymney line to Quakers Yard.

Latterly the old Taff Vale Plymouth Road station, which lies south-west of High Street, has been used as a goods station by both TV and B&M/LNW trains. Access from the branch is by a spur from Ynysfach Junction and a reversal.

THE DOWLAIS BRANCH

This very short (1½ mile) branch begins at Pant, where there is a low-level platform for Dowlais trains; this is however not always used, the branch train being loaded in the main platform and reversed at the junction. Running over the LNWR Morlais Tunnel, and passing the former junction for the extensive Morlais Castle Quarries sidings, we pass again over the tunnel and then over the LNW in the open, to Pantyscallog (Upper) station and Ivor Junction where a loop, not used for passenger trains, runs to Penywern Junction of the LNW. There are extensive sidings on the east side, including that of ICI Ltd, before arriving at Dowlais, renamed Central in 1924, a single platform with a crude one-storey building.

THE RHYMNEY BRANCH

Following the completion of the main line, the northern section of the 'Old Rumney' became little more than a colliery siding, though enough traffic developed to enable the branch to be doubled. The branch began at Aberbargoed Junction, a mile north of Pengam; there was a colliery halt at this junction. Aberbargoed station (1 m.) was a conditional stop for many years; the present station dates from 1935, but is in fact a refurbishment of the first station; the second station proved badly sited and was closed and sold in 1935. It was called Aberbargoed until 1905 and after 1924; Aber Bargoed & Bargoed 1905–9, and Bargoed & Aberbargoed 1909–24. Further up, a platform erected beside the Coedymoeth Colliery was the first Cwmsifiog station; in 1937 a new one was built half a mile north nearer the town and the old one left for miners.

The Bassaleg Viaduct seen as it was in May 1974.   *Lens of Sutton*

A train headed by locomotive No. 17, crossing the great Cefn Viaduct about 1922.
L.C.G.B., Ken Nunn Collection

There was another halt at Elliot Pits, before reaching New Tredegar station (3 m.). This was called White Rose until 1885; New Tredegar colliery had been built in 1853 near to the village called White Rose. From 1906 to 1924 the station was called New Tredegar & Tyrphil (the latter being a village on the other side of the valley, served by the Rhymney Railway) A short distance north was New Tredegar Colliery Halt, opened in 1901. Here the valley side was unstable, due to a seam of quicksand some 40 ft down; there was a big slip in 1905 and another in 1928; during the single line working resulting from this, a fatal collision occurred between a miners' train of Powell Duffryn carriages and an ordinary train. Finally on 11th April, 1930 the whole valley side collapsed, taking with it much of the colliery plant. Three days later the GWR decided not to attempt to re-open; the colliery had already been closed. The McLaren Collieries were further up the valley, and to serve these a spur was run from the Rhymney Railway at Tyrphil, on an embankment of spoil, to the other side of the valley. Abertysswg station (4¾ m.) was abandoned; it had been opened in 1905. The McLaren's No. 1 Halt probably remained in use; however Rhymney station, beside McLaren No. 2, was closed.

The B&M Rhymney station (5¾ m.) comprised a single platform, though it once had a turntable and small engine shed. It was sited at Pwll Uchaf, a mile from the town, and was called Rhymney (Lower) or sometimes Rhymney (Pwll Uchaf). The reason for this was that the Old Rumney had met the private railway from Rhymney Ironworks at this point. This tramway remained in use and later also served Maerdy Colliery. However, from 1st March, 1933 all the tracks around Pwll Uchaf were closed down.

The spur line from Tyrphil remained in use until the McLaren's Colliery closed in 1969, and for some time after on clearance work. The Elliot Pits, which were on the section of the branch between Aberbargoed and New Tredegar, which remained in use after the landslide, closed in 1967.

THE CAERPHILLY BRANCH

When this was only a freight line, running 3¾ miles from Machen to an end-on junction with the Rhymney half a mile east of Caerphilly station, it chiefly served a works at ½ m. Tin Works Junction, 1 m. Rock Veins Siding, and 1¾ m. Rhos Llantwit Colliery, apart from through traffic mainly from Pontypool. The opening of the PC&N Machen Loop has already been described; this ran from just west of Machen to Gwaunabara Junction. In connection with the railcar developments, halts were opened at White Hart in 1947 (closed 30th June, 1952), which had platforms on both the old line and the loop, with a road in between; at Waterloo, which had a platform only on the up side; and Fountain Bridge, on the down side only. At Gwernydomen Halt, which was close to Gwaunanbara Junction, the lines had come together and trains in both directions called. These were not, however, B&M trains; though B&M engines mostly worked the freight trains, the passenger trains were either Great Western or AD&R.

A general view of Dowlais Central on 13th September, 1951.   *R.W. Rush*

A busy scene at Dowlais Central station in 1922. The 0−6−0T engines are believed to be Nos. 17 and 18.   *L.C.G.B., Ken Nunn Collection*

Dowlais Top station as viewed on 23rd August, 1961.   *E. Wilmshurst*

The 11.15 am Newport to Brecon local service seen here at Dowlais Top station on 23rd August, 1961.   *E. Wilmshurst*

A poor but important view of Dowlais Top station about 1900; the LNWR crossed over
the line by the bridge seen beyond the crossing gates.   *Locomotive Publishing Co.*

The junction between the LNWR and B&M railways at Dowlais Top, just east of the
station.   *E.J. Miller*

Pantyscallog High Level Halt, facing Dowlais Central viewed from a train in 1957.
H.C. Casserley

The short Pantywaun platform on 30th November, 1957, looking south again seen from a train. Note the height of the station above the surrounding countryside.
R.M. Casserley

The slide at New Tredegar Colliery on 11th April, 1930; this portion of the B&M Rhymney Branch was never re-opened; service was cut back to New Tredegar station, and collieries further up the valley served by a spur from the Rhymney Railway; photographed on 13th April, 1930, the day before the line was officially closed.

British Railways

A view of Fochriw station in September 1918 showing clearly the staggered up and down platforms. *Lens of Sutton*

An enchanting 1920s postcard view of Deri and Darran station.

Lens of Sutton

On the footplate of No. 3706 at Pengam station (south end) waiting to proceed whilst No. 4238 can be seen in the distance, on 18th April, 1962.   *H.B. Priestley*

Maesycymmer station looking north in 1912 showing the Vale of Neath viaduct dominating the scene.   *Lens of Sutton*

An early view of Fleur-de-Lis Halt.   *Lens of Sutton*

Fleur-de-Lis Halt in July 1956; note the GWR 'pagoda' type station building.

H.C. Casserley

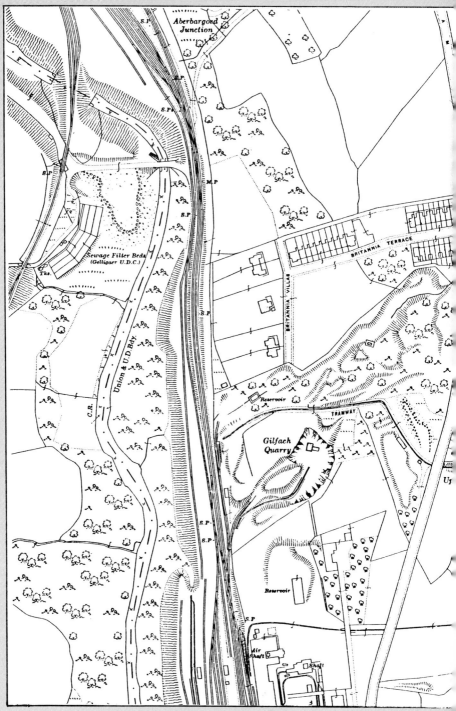

The B&M south of Aberbargoed Junction in 1901; at the top the connection to the Rhymney Railway runs to the left and the former 'Old Rumney' runs straight on.
Reproduced from the 1901, 25″ Ordnance Survey map

The view from a Newport train headed by No. 3706 at Bedwas in April 1962. Note the somersault signal.   *H.B. Priestley*

New Tredegar station seen from the south on 10th July, 1958 with a train about to leave for Newport headed by No. 9482.   *H.C. Casserley*

Trethomas station looking towards Bedwas, about 1950, dominated by the colliery in the background.   *Locomotive Publishing Co.*

A superb early view of Machen station photographed at the east end of the station.
Lens of Sutton

The remains of Machen Locomotive Works in 1949.   *H.C. Casserley*

A view of Machen station on 13th July, 1951 with 0–6–0PT No. 3770 about to leave
on a local service.   *R.W. Rush*

Machen station looking west, with the Caerphilly branch curving-off to the left of the main line. *H.C. Casserley*

The west end of Machen station *c*1910, showing AD&R steam railcar on the Caerphilly branch. *R.W. Kidner Collection*

Brecon & Merthyr somersault signals at Bedwas (looking east) on 27th August, 1950
(*left*) and a distant somersault signal at Newport still in place in 1974 (*right*).

Oakwood Collection

Church Road station as seen on 6th May, 1974, when the station buildings were a private dwelling. *Lens of Sutton*

A view looking east at Bassaleg station with No. 3706 on the 7.35 am ex Brecon waiting to depart on 18th April, 1962. *H.B. Priestley*

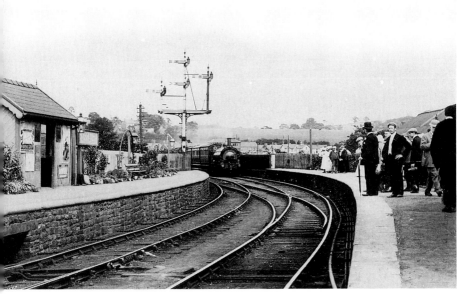

A busy scene at Bassaleg station looking towards Newport, about 1910. The signals are
worthy of a glance. *Author's Collection*

0−6−0PT No. 3706 at Bassaleg station (looking north) on 18th April, 1962.
H.B. Priestley

An early view of Rhiwderin village showing the railway station bottom left.

Lens of Sutton

Rhiwderin station looking west on 3rd July, 1949.   *Locomotive Publishing Co.*

Chapter Fifteen
The Grouping and After

Industrial conditions in South Wales were already changing fast when the independent existence of the B&M came to an end. Closure of many of the historic ironworks in the Dowlais–Merthyr area, the prolonged depression in the coalfield, and the rapid development of road transport following World War I, all hit the local railways hard. The removal of competition between railways – especially between the GWR and LMS following the traffic-pooling agreement of 1933 – also reduced the volume of traffic exchanged at Talyllyn. The Rhymney branch, on which trouble had often been encountered due to earth movements on the hillside north of New Tredegar, was partially closed for a time from this cause during World War I, and a more serious landslip in 1928 followed by another in April 1930, eventually brought about the complete closure of the 2½ miles between New Tredegar and Rhymney as from 14th April, 1930. By this time the only colliery working on the branch could be served from the parallel branch of the former Rhymney Railway, without recourse to the costly litigation in which the B&M and the RR had engaged over this question 30 years before! Following this closure, the former B&M Rhymney branch was reduced to single track between Aberbargoed Junction and New Tredegar, and the rest of it was abandoned.

A fatal passenger train accident occurred at New Tredegar on 9th October, 1928, while single line working was in operation due to a landslip and all traffic was being worked over the up line. An up passenger train overran signals and collided with a colliers' train, one passenger being killed.

The whole timetable in the early 'thirties was somewhat reduced. There were four trains on the main line between Brecon and Newport, with four from Newport to New Tredegar plus two from Maesycwmmer to New Tredegar, one from Fochriew to Bargoed and one from Dowlais Top to Bargoed. The Pant–Dowlais service had seven trains, and Pontsticill–Merthyr five plus some LMS trains over the Abergavenny line. On the Caerphilly branch there were three trains through from Newport, and five railmotor workings between Caerphilly and Machen.

At Brecon the Johnson 0–4–4Ts on the Hereford–Swansea trains were now seen in LMS livery, but not for long; in 1931 the trains from Hereford ceased to run beyond Brecon, and the Great Western put on a service from Brecon to Neath, thus restoring something that had ceased 60 years earlier.

The weather continued to cause disruption in most winters. There was an especially bad snow-storm from 25th–28th January, 1939, and a tank engine became stuck in an eight-foot drift at Torpantau; two engines sent to help were also stuck for two hours. On the 27th, trains from Brecon only ran to Dowlais as the main line was blocked at Pantywaun.

Many of the 47 B&M engines taken over by the GWR in 1922 were very run-down through sheer hard work, and seven of them were withdrawn in the first year of the new ownership, the ex-LSWR 4–4–2T not even surviving long enough to bear her GWR number. The 2–4–0Ts were all withdrawn without alteration, but some interesting modifications were carried out to various of the other survivors. Neither of the two old Sharp, Stewart saddle tanks Nos. 17 and 18 were reboilered, but both were fitted with pannier tanks. Nos. 8 and 14 of the 1884–6 series saddle tanks were also rebuilt as panniers, No. 8 with a GWR boiler; four out of the five of the 1890–1900 series were also given pannier tanks, and three of them (Nos. 22, 28, and 29) had GWR '2301-class' boilers fitted. No. 29 (GWR 2173) was fitted with a totally enclosed cab. One of the ex-GWR saddle tanks, B&M No. 33 (GWR 1693), was similarly treated to an enclosed cab on return to the parent company; all three engines of this series were also converted to pannier tanks, No. 1685 (B&M 32) being the only one to receive a superheater.

The four Vulcan-built long-boiler 0–6–2STs, Nos. 19, 20, 23, and 26, were not very popular with the GWR, but after her three companion engines had all been withdrawn by 1925, No. 20 survived, as GWR No. 1677, until 1928, virtually unchanged except for GW boiler fittings. The whole of her 'Great Western' life was spent on the Cambrian Section at Machynlleth, mostly on banking duties over Talerddig Summit.

All of Dunbar's 14 modern 0–6–2T were reboilered from 1923 onwards with GWR or ex-Rhymney Railway boilers. It was appropriate that of the 13 former B&M locomotives which passed into British Railways stock on 1st January, 1948, the last two survivors were ex-B&M Nos. 49 and 50, which had also been the last two engines delivered to the old company. As BR Nos. 1668 and 1670 they were withdrawn in February 1954, having outlived the Brecon & Merthyr Railway by 32 years.

After Grouping, a variety of GWR locomotive types gradually superseded the native products on the B&M section, including Dean and Collett 0–6–0 goods tender engines; pannier, 0–6–2 and 2–6–2 side tanks, and even 2–8–0Ts on the coal train workings at the Newport end. Ex-Cambrian 0–6–0 goods engines also made their appearance on the Brecon–Newport trains.

The Dean '2301' class 0–6–0s were a familiar sight at Brecon for more than 30 years. They were put on the Mid-Wales trains immediately after Grouping, and it was convenient for some to be rostered for turns to Newport. When the Collett type arrived, it was not so simple; it was not allowed on the Mid-Wales north of Three Cocks due to weak bridges. For this reason the '2301' class went on being used between Moat Lane and Brecon into the late 'fifties, until a suitable replacement could be found. This was the Ivatt '2MT' 2–6–0, a standard BR design, light enough for the Mid-Wales, and also very useful on the B&M line. Pannier tanks were mainly used on the Neath line; these also were forbidden on the Mid-Wales; however they frequently worked the Newport trains.

At Brecon, the GWR shared the engine shed with the LMS, and after the old Midland 0–4–4Ts started to fade away on the Hereford trains, they were replaced by LNWR radial 0–6–2Ts and later ex-Lancashire & Yorkshire 0–6–0s.

At Nationalisation, the following GWR engines were shedded at Brecon: Nos. 2345/51, 2523/69, 3638, 3706/67, 5801, 9614. At Merthyr there were: Nos. 333, 1878, 2760, 4632/5, 5654/77/78/98, 5711/21/69, 6408/27/34, 7717/66/72, 8736, 9618/22/38/43. However engines from almost any shed from Oswestry down to Cardiff were liable to find themselves on some part of the B&M lines.

Maesycymmer B&M station (facing north) with a train crossing on the Vale of Neath viaduct on 10th July, 1958.   *H.C. Casserley*

A general view of Torpantau station looking north.   *Lens of Sutton*

An official report in June 1947 stated that ex-B&M locomotives Nos. 36–43 and 45–50 were still at work. Nos. 38 and 40–43 were at Radyr shed, 39 at Rhymney, 36–7 and 46–7 at Cardiff East Dock. The other four were probably stored. In the 1920s the GWR still needed heavy tank engines to move coal, and had reboilered the '36' class with GWR tapered boilers from 1924 on, or in the case of Nos. 504, 698 and 1113, with boilers from the Rhymney 'R' class which was very similar. The '45' class also received new boilers, No. 1670 being somewhat of an oddity in having a Rhymney boiler but retaining its B&M smokebox and chimney. The last of the '36' class went in 1951 and the last '45' three years later. Some other engines, including Nos. 17, 18, and 22–9 were given pannier tanks in place of saddle tanks.

With the arrival at Brecon in 1953 of the first of the Ivatt '2MT 2–6–0s (an LM '2P' 2–6–0 had been tried out as early as 1950), the Brecon to Newport service was confirmed as a tender-engine run, already largely worked by Dean and Collett 0–6–0s. Although the B&M had set its face against tender engines, they did prove useful on this service. There had never been water-points at Brecon except at the Watton shed, and in 'tank' days engines had watered at Bargoed and at Talybont; the tender engines proved able to cut out the latter watering.

After nationalisation, there was an initial spurt in through holiday trains from South Wales to Pwllheli, where Butlins had built a great new holiday camp. This began to die away later, however, as more workers became able to afford a car. One small new traffic was in troop trains to a National Service camp set up at Sennybridge on the Neath line; most of these came via Hereford and Three Cocks and thus only used the B&M between Talyllyn and Brecon; they were worked mainly by pairs of 0–6–0PTs from Cardiff shed. Somewhat later, in 1958, a longer stretch of track benefited from the removal of regular trains of ammonia liquid from Dowlais to Durham from the Brynmawr and Abergavenny route, which was closed, and their re-routing to one via the B&M line, Talyllyn East Loop and Hereford. Again pairs of pannier tanks were used and on one occasion a pair was noted hauling 36 full tanks up to Torpantau.

By the mid-1950s there were still four trains per day down the length of the main line between Brecon and Newport. There were also a number of short workings for workmen: between Bargoed and Dowlais Central, and trains to New Tredegar commencing at Pengam, Maesycwmmer or Bedwas. There were in fact nine trains on the New Tredegar branch. The Merthyr branch had two trains, plus one between Cefn Coed and Merthyr only, which was a school train and ran in term-time only.

On 23rd May, 1951 an interesting ceremony took place at Talyllyn; the unveiling of a plaque commemorating the 135 years of the tunnel, as part of the local Festival of Britain celebrations. The idea had been put forward by Mr J.C.P. de Winton; the author of this book, at the time Public Relations Officer for British Railways and also a member of the Newcomen Society, took part in the work leading up to the event. It was widely promoted as the oldest working railway tunnel in the world. However, the Chief Regional Officer of the Western Region, on whose patch it was, struck a dissenting note. He wrote ' . . . in addition to lowering the tunnel by four feet, it was

...lais Central station on 29th May,
...3 with GWR No. 337 (ex TVR loco-
...ive) about to leave with the 4.10 pm
...ice to Pant station.   *W.A. Camwell*

...700 class 0−6−0PT hauling the
...ection Saloon at Dowlais Top
...on in July 1954.   *N. Leek*

...unusual view of Talybont water
...er and station buildings in the
...0s.   *Lens of Sutton*

also heightened by about four feet. From this it is clear that it must have been widened ... you will appreciate that the claim that it is the oldest railway tunnel in the world cannot be substantiated'. However, a good time was had and the plaque was unveiled by John Davies JP of Brecon, who had joined the B&M as a cleaner 75 years earlier.

The ordinary passenger service on the Pant–Dowlais branch was withdrawn on 28th June, 1952; however the workmens' service continued. It was not until November 1959 that British Railways announced its intention of closing the branch entirely. There were now three workmens' trains per weekday and two on Saturdays, and two scheduled freight trains between Dowlais Central and Pontsticill. There was one complication; Pantyscallog Halt (High Level) was the subject of a 1916 Deed between Merthyr Junction Railway Co. and one Lt Edward Davies, which provided that the halt could only be closed on the payment to Davies of £40, which sum he had contributed to the construction. Unfortunately Lt Davies or his heirs could not be traced. The argument for closure was presented in a way which became familiar; to the staff costs of £2,800 were added £533 for repairs to rolling stock, £806 for fuel and water, and other items not quantified; the passenger revenue was put at only £373. It was proposed that the sidings of Guest Keen Iron & Steel Co. Ltd and ICI Ltd be retained and this freight service would continue. Rock Siding and the loop line to the now-closed Abergavenny Line were required for a road. In 1960 notices were posted announcing the ending of the service on 2nd May (Monday) but in fact the service worked all that week, trains running to Bargoed. On the Friday, the 2.25 pm train from Brecon to Newport was in error turned onto the Dowlais branch at Pant, due to signalling work, and had to reverse.

At the Bassaleg end of the line, Church Road was reduced to a halt on 15th September, 1952, and Rhiwderin was closed for passenger and parcels traffic on 1st March, 1952. The Machen–Pontypridd service (never worked by the B&M) was withdrawn on 15th September, 1956.

The 'Beeching Axe' now began to swing. As services were threatened, objections came in from District and County Councils all over South and Mid-Wales. The strongest came in regard to the proposed closing of the Mid-Wales and Brecon & Merthyr lines. A Llanidloes councillor blamed much of the decline in traffic on the withdrawal of through trains down these lines; he himself had to travel to Cardiff via Shrewsbury and Hereford as no connecting trains via Talyllyn could get him there for lunch time. A sensible proposal was put up for a fast railcar service omitting most stations and halts from Moat Lane via Talyllyn to South Wales, with Brecon in effect on a branch line, but no notice was taken of this.

There followed in quick succession passenger withdrawals between Merthyr and Pontsticill Junction (13th November, 1961), both the 'main line' between Newport (exclusive) and Brecon and the New Tredegar branch (31st December, 1962); while simultaneous withdrawals between Hereford–Brecon and Moat Lane–Brecon on the last-named date left the Breconshire county town without any railway passenger service, the Neath & Brecon trains having already been taken off on 15th October, 1962. This left the Caerphilly–Machen–Newport unadvertised workmen's service as the last passenger trains on the B&M, until their withdrawal on 1st July, 1963, in conjunction with the closure of Caerphilly Works.

Closures for freight traffic took place between Deri Junction and Pant Junction, on 5th August, 1963, and between Brecon and Merthyr, also Pontsticill–Dowlais Central, on 4th May, 1964; Brecon survived as a non-rail-connected coal depot until 9th November, 1964. In January 1963 there had been a short suspension of B&M goods services to Brecon due to a very large body of ice hanging in Torpantau tunnel. There was a 'last run' special from Cardiff to Brecon on 2nd May, 1964, comprising 2–6–2T No. 4555 and 0–6–0PT No. 3690 with six coaches, a few days before lifting began at Pontsticill.

When the Merthyr Branch was lifted, 1¾ miles of track northwards from Rhydycar Junction was left in place to serve the Vaynor Quarries; the private railway joined by a reversal at the north end, and a line also ran under the former B&M to a works on the east side.

Machen to Bedwas Colliery was singled and worked as a siding from 27th January, 1964, the line north thereof to Pengam having been closed on 31st December, 1962. Meanwhile, the Caerphilly–Machen branch continued to be used for through freight trains to and from Newport; from 20th July, 1964 these used the down line via Fountain Bridge as a single line, the more easily-graded up line via Waterloo being closed to avoid maintaining the bridge over the Rhymney River. Diversion of these through trains via Radyr and Cardiff later enabled the Caerphilly–Machen section to be closed entirely from 20th November, 1967; from this date Bassaleg Junction to Bedwas Colliery was worked as a siding.

These 10½ miles of single track constituted the only surviving segment of the B&M in BR operation, catering for substantial flows of traffic from Bedwas Colliery (principally to the Nantgarw Coke Ovens); coal into the British Benzole & Coal Distillation plant at Trethomas; and stone ballast from Powell Duffryn Quarries Ltd, Machen Quarry, for use in various Western Region engineering divisions. This section of the former B&M, originally part of the historic 'Old Rumney', was no longer connected with the Western Valleys line at Bassaleg Junction, but ran parallel with it as a separate single line to Park Junction, Newport. Traffic returns over this section showed about 250,000 tonnes of rail ballast annually from the Machen Quarries of Powell Duffryn, and some 100,000 tonnes of coal per annum going into the works at British Benzol and Coal Distillation Ltd at Trethomas. In addition, some 100,000 tonnes of coal was sent each year from Bedwas Colliery to Nantgarw.

The Elliot Pits in the Rhymney Valley, by this time served from the former Rhymney Railway branch at Tyr Phil, finally closed in 1967, and McLaren's in 1969. Since the closing of Coedymoeth Colliery in 1910, and the abandonment of the New Tredegar due to a landslide in 1930, the valley had much changed and landscaping of spoil has covered traces of most that was once there.

The railways through the Valleys were very much part of the coal industry, and the two industries have declined together, though the railways suffered heavily under the Beeching axe before the final rationalisation of the world coal market forced a drastic reduction in Welsh mines, which were never geographically suited to high mechanisation. In 1990 there is still rail freight up the Sirhowy Valley as far as Markham, and the west side of the Rhymney Valley still has a passenger service. There is a passenger line too through Merthyr Vale, and freight trains run to Merthyr via Cwm Bargoed. Further south, freight trains run from Newport up to Bedwas over the former B&M and over the old Sirhowy route to Tredegar. So as often happens, it is the oldest lines that survive. The frenetic activity of the boom years of mining for Welsh coal, which gave the countryside more railways than it could possibly need for any other purpose, have left a scarred waste in many places which only decades of effort to create new industries can efface.

Nevertheless it was an era which will never be forgotten. The Brecon & Merthyr earned for its servants and proprietors little financial reward, but it created a tradition, character, and history that were in many ways unique. Like Crawshay Bailey's engine, it even had its own song, the chorus of which conjures up a last picture of two double-framed saddle tanks toiling into the hills and, bringing up the rear perhaps, a brake-van with lace curtains painted on the side-lights:

> Six and five times up to Dowlais,
> Six and five times back same way,
> Whenever I wass finish, I wass get no extra pay!

A fine view of No. 4, 0–6–0ST on a very mixed goods train at LLwyncelyn signal box on 12th August, 1913.   *L.C.G.B., Ken Nunn Collection*

Chapter Sixteen

What Remains Today?

Soon after closing, Brecon Free Street became a Driving Instruction Centre and was later demolished, to become a fire station. Watton became a site for Welsh Water offices. Talybont however was extended to become an Outdoor Centre for school children.

At Talyllyn the tunnel still exists, but is boarded up: the south side buildings are a house, though part of the platform has been left and the relief platform on the north loop is still there, but probably not for long. At Talybont the station house is in good order and much of the platforms left; the bridges still cross the road and canal, but that over the Usk has gone. Torpantau station site is used for animal pens.

The plaque which had been attached to the tunnel in 1951 was rescued by the Breconshire Railway Society and lodged in the Brecon Museum. It reads:

TALYLLYN TUNNEL
674 yards
OPENED BY THE HAY RAILWAY
7 May 1816
John Hodgkinson Engineer
ENLARGED AND RE-OPENED BY THE
BRECON AND MERTHYR RAILWAY
1 May 1863
Henry Conybeare Engineer
This plaque was set up by the Brecon Chamber of Trade
in the year of the Festival of Britain – 1951

At Ponsticill the single storey building on the old main platform exists, and the lower part of the signal box, which is being incorporated into a house. The narrow gauge track of the Brecon Mountain Railway ends between the old station and the lake. This continues south almost entirely on the old formation to Pant, the station buildings of which are demolished, though the platforms are in situ. The new narrow gauge station is 30 yds away to the west, and the tracks regain the B&M formation near the bridge just north of the old station.

Pentir Rhiw remained, adapted by the Royal Navy as a training centre for HMS Collingwood at Portsmouth. Torpantau was demolished though a few platform remnants remained. Dolygaer remained, for use by Boy Scouts.

Some of the bridges on this section remained: over the canal at Talybont, at Cefn-y-Cwmmer, and Pontsarn, which is now part of the Brecon National Park. The bridge over the Usk at Talybont was demolished, however.

Only a few remnants of the south end of Ivor Junction can be traced, the new Heads of the Valley A470 road having obliterated most of it. However at Dowlais Central the stone goods shed is in excellent condition, being used as a youth centre; the main building also exists but boarded up. The Dowlais Top area is much changed owing to the new Heads of the Valleys road; southwards through Pantywaun there is a vast area of open-cast mining.

Further south much remains: Rhymney station, the platforms at Trethomas, Machen station now a house; Rhiwderin station and contents now the property of the Caerphilly Railway Society. New Tredegar station became a childrens' play area.

The former PC&N section is now difficult to follow; the tunnel under the line at White Hart has gone, and the area around Fountain Bridge Halt has reverted to forest.

A Proserpine Mountain Railway train from Peat arriving at Pontetizzll in August 1986 hauled by Am June 1961 of 1908 Graf Schwerin-Lowitz.

Appendix One
The Brecon Mountain Railway

As early as 1972 an engineer looking for a suitable site for a railway on which to run renovated narrow-gauge engines lit upon the Pant to Torpantau section of the B&M, then disused for only eight years, and set about negotiating the purchase of parcels of track land which had been sold. Planning permission was obtained from the National Park, and a Light Railway Order applied for in 1980. Workshops were set up at Pant, west of the old station and a large car park laid out. Track was laid between there and Pontsticill, 1¾ miles, in old 75 lb. rail, set at 1 ft 11¾ in. gauge.

The following locomotives were obtained:

Name	Type	Maker	Makers' No.	Built
	0–4–0WT	Orenstein & Koppel	12722	1936
Graf Schwerin-Lowitz	0–6–2WT	Jung	1261	1908
Sybil	0–4–0ST	Hunslet	827	1903
	4–6–2	Baldwin	61269	1930

Carriages were built on frames obtained from South Africa.

Service began on 8th June, 1980 between Ponsticill and Pant, though plans were announced for extensions skirting the Taf Fechan reservoir and then rising above Pentwyn reservoir up to Torpantau, to a terminus at Glyn Collwyn just beyond the tunnel.

At Torpantau the road has been re-aligned to remove a right-angled turn after passing under the railway, and extension of the BMR would require a skew bridge over the new road, provision for which was made when the roadworks were carried out.

The track does not exactly follow the former B&M; owing to one landowner being unwilling to sell, some 600 yds near Pant had to be laid on a new alignment. The 1989 timetables comprised seven trains each way in peak season, daily, and working on four days off-peak. The fare included admission to the workshop at Pant. There is no road access to Pontsticill station.

In 1989 the BMR took over the narrow gauge Vale of Rheidol railway from Aberystwyth to Devils Bridge in Ceredigion, following its sale by British Rail, and the Pant workshop is being used in 1990 to rebuild one of the three engines from this line.

No. 2247 waiting at Newport with the 8.03 am service to Brecon on 23rd August, 1961.   E. Wilmshurst

No. 18, 0−6−0ST taking water at Pant station in 1922. *L.C.G.B., Ken Nunn Collection*

B&M 0−6−2T locomotive No. 23 (long boilered type) at Merthyr station.
Author's Collection

The goods working timetable for October 1902

For the Information of the Company's Servants only.

BRECON & MERTHYR RAILWAY

WORKING TIME TABLE

FOR

BRECON & MERTHYR

RAILWAY—COMPANY'S GOODS, MINERAL

AND COLLIERS' TRAINS,

ON

RUMNEY & BRECON SECTIONS.

OCTOBER, 1902

AND UNTIL FURTHER NOTICE.

CONTENTS:

	PAGE.
Special Instructions	2
Time Table, Bassaleg Section—Up Trains	4
Do. Do. Down Trains	6
Do. Brecon Section	8
McLaren Colliers' Train	10
P. D. Co.'s Machen Colliers' Train	12

SPECIAL INSTRUCTIONS.

Stationmasters, Signalmen, Guards, Engine-drivers, and others must use every effort to ensure the running of these Trains to the booked times as shewn herein.

Working of Trains over the Line.

It is important that the Signalmen should ascertain the running of the different trains with a view to working them over the line in accordance with Booked Time.

The Signalman at each Tablet or Block Station must therefore make the best use of the Telegraph or Telephone to ascertain how the trains are running so as to avoid delay as far as possible.

Picking Up and Putting Off Traffic.

Guards must be careful to see that their trains are properly protected by Signals when shunting or standing on the Main line, and when shunting to and from Sidings and Main line.

Traffic is to be put off, or taken on, at the request of any Stationmaster or Signalman, whether the train is appointed in the Time Tables to stop at the place in question or not ; but any Special Service must be reported on the back of Guard's Journal, and sent to the Manager's Office on the day following.

Guards working over Rhymney Section and Caerphilly Branch, and Bargoed Branch must obtain permits for all traffic in owners' wagons conveyed in their Trains, unless arranged otherwise. The Permits to be taken care of and handed to the Stationmaster or person in charge, where the traffic is put off. Such traffic received without Permits must be reported to the Manager's Office.

Traffic for Collieries and other Private Sidings.

When Guards have traffic to put off at any Colliery or other Private Siding, they must inform the Station Master who has charge of the siding the number and owner of each wagon, what it contains and where labelled from, on form No. 217 provided for the purpose.

Cases have recently come under notice in which guards have omitted to advise the Stationmasters of wagons put off at collieries and other private sidings, with the result that demurrage has accrued on the wagons before being cleared. It is of the utmost importance that guards should rigidly carry out this instruction and agents must watch this matter very carefully and report any case in which this instruction is not complied with.

Private Owners' Wagons.

Stationmasters and guards must make every exertion to prevent detention of Private Wagons at stations or sidings. All such wagons should be properly and fully labelled ; and the loaded wagons, especially for inland stations, should show the route on the labels, as well as the names of the stations, in clear, unmistakable characters.

SPEED OF TRAINS,
Working Up and Down Heavy Inclines, and Pinning-Down Brakes.

In working Goods and Mineral Trains over the heavy portions of the line between Talyllyn and Bargoed, the following instructions must be observed :— In going up a bank, when two engines are employed, one engine is to be placed at the rear of the train ; and if three engines are employed, two must be in front and one behind. In descending the incline it is best to have the engine power in front. Care must be taken, when working an engine at the rear of a train, that the speed at which it is run does not exceed 14 miles per hour.

The greatest caution and vigilance must be observed by Enginemen, Guards, and Brakesmen in working down inclines, and the following instructions must be attended to :—

Working between Brecon and Dowlais, and Pantywaen and Bargoed Junction.

Passenger Trains—Maximum Speed—25 miles per hour. Goods Trains—Maximum Speed—14 miles per hour.

The brakes of all wagons must be carefully examined by the Guards.

Goods trains from Pontsticill must stop at the north end of Torpantau Tunnel ; and those from Talyllyn at the south end of Torpantau Tunnel to pin down the brakes.

Guards of all Down Mineral trains must pin down the wagon brakes before leaving any station or siding between Rhymney and Fleur-de-lis, and stop at Fluer-de-lis to pick them up.

All Goods and Mineral trains must reduce speed to two miles per hour before descending the incline at Pennorth Bridge, and also at Maypole Bridge, to allow the guards to pin down the wagon brakes ; and the brakesman to ride on engine from Machen to top of incline, so as to be in from of train ready to apply the brakes. When the driver has satisfied himself that a sufficient number of brakes has been applied, he must intimate it to the guards by sounding his whistle, see page 37 of Appendix, dated November 1st, 1897.

Trains must not be run at a greater speed than SIX MILES per hour through Fluer-de-lis Yard, and past Machen Loco. Shops.

NOTE—(a) An Up Goods Train must not pass Pentir-Rhiw Signal Box at a greater speed than six miles an hour, and an Up Passenger Train 15 miles an hour.

In the case of a Down Train which has not to cross an Up Train at Pentir-Rhiw, the Tablets can be exchanged without stopping the trains in the Loop, but the Speed must not exceed, in the case of a Goods Train, 10 miles an hour, and of a Passenger Train, 15 miles an hour, when passing the Signal Box.

(b) G.W. Down Trains are allowed to run through Maesycwmmer Junction at a speed not exceeding 15 miles an hour to enable them to get up the Branch.

In addition to the above Special Instructions, all Officers and Servants of the Company must give their careful attention to the Instructions and Regulations contained in the Appendix to the Working Time Table, dated 1st November, 1897.

Traffic Manager's Office,
Newport, Sept, 1902.
M—715—600

JOHN GALL.

Traffic Manager

BETWEEN BASSALEG, RHYMNEY, & PONTSTICILL.

UP TRAINS.

STATIONS.	1 4.30 a.m. T.I. Co.'s Empties arr. / dep.	2 5.45 a.m. P.D. Empties arr. / dep.	3 6.15 a.m. Thro' Goods arr. / dep.	4 a.m. Guest,Keen & Co's Col. Train arr. / dep.	5 a.m. G.W. Goods arr. / dep.	6 7.10 a.m. Mix. Goods & Empties arr. / dep.	7 9.0 a.m. Rhymney Goods arr. / dep.	8 10.30 a.m. C.B. Train arr. / dep.	9 a.m. G.W. Goods arr. / dep.	10 11.30 a.m. Bargoed Branch Goods arr. / dep.	11 11.45 a.m. Colliery Empties arr. / dep.
BASSALEG	... 4 30	... 5 45	... 6 15	...	...	...	...	...	...	...	... 11 45
Rhiwderin	...	...	...	...	...	...	...	...	...	...	...
Church Road	...	...	...	...	...	...	...	...	...	...	...
Machen Line Kilns	...	...	...	...	...	...	...	...	...	...	...
Machen	4 40 5 0	6 5 6 10	... 6 35	...	...	7 30 7 40	9 20 9 40	10 55 11 5	...	...	... 12 5
Machen Forge	...	...	...	...	...	...	...	11 35	...	...	...
Rudry Sidings	...	...	...	...	...	...	...	11 40 11 50	...	...	...
Caerphilly	...	...	...	...	...	...	...	12 0	...	...	...
Bedwas	5 10	... 6 20	6 43	...	...	7 50 7 55	9 50 9 55	12 10	...	...	... 12 15
Bryngwyn Siding	...	...	...	...	...	...	...	...	...	...	...
Maesycwmmer	5 35 5 30	6 42	7 5	...	...	8 15	10 15 10 30	...	...	...	...
Maesycwmmer Junct	6 21	...	...	...	...	8 20	...	...	...	...	...
Fleur-de-lis	0 45	6 50 6 55	...	...	7 15 7 20 7 30	8 25 8 35	10 35 11 0 11 5 11 10	...	11 15 11 20	...	12 40 12 45
Pengam	...	...	...	...	7 15 7 30	8 40 8 50	11 13 11 20	...	...	...	...
Gilfach Colliery	... 6 31	...	...	...	...	...	...	...	...	...	...
Gilfach Quarry	...	7 0	...	...	...	...	...	...	...	...	...
Aberbargoed Junct	...	...	...	...	7 45	8 55	11 23	...	11 38	...	12 55
Gwaelodywain Colliery	...	...	...	...	...	...	...	...	...	...	...
Lord Tredegar's Siding	...	...	...	...	...	...	...	...	...	...	...
Aberbargoed Station	...	7 20	7 42 8 2	...	...	...	...	...	...	...	...
Elliot Pit	6 46	...	...	...	...	9 10	11 38	...	...	...	...
Whiterose Colliery	...	...	...	...	...	...	...	...	...	...	...
Whiterose	6 50	7 25 7 35	8 22	...	8 0 8 10	9 15 9 25	11 42 12 4	...	11 50 12 25	...	1 15
New Derlwyn Colliery	...	...	...	...	...	9 32	...	...	...	...	...
New Tredegar Pit	...	...	...	...	...	9 45	...	...	...	...	...
McLaren No. 1	7 0 7 15	7 48 8 0	...	...	8 30	9 50	12 25	...	12 33	...	...
RHYMNEY	7 20	8 5	8 35	...	8 35	...	12 30	12 33	...	...	...
FLEUR-DE-LIS	...	...	...	...	...	...	...	...	...	...	...
Pengam	...	...	7 15	6 25	...	...	...	...	...	11 30	...
Bargoed Junction	...	...	7 8 7 20	...	...	...	...	...	...	11 37 11 42	...
Darran Pit	...	...	7 31	...	...	...	...	...	...	11 52 12 5	...
Darran	...	...	...	6 31	...	...	...	...	...	...	...
Deri Junction	...	...	...	6 37	...	...	...	...	...	12 20	...
Fochriw	...	...	7 42	6 45	...	...	...	...	...	12 30	...
Fochriw Pit Junct	...	...	8 2	...	...	...	...	...	...	...	...
Pantywaen	...	...	...	6 50	...	...	...	...	...	...	...
Rhymney I.C. Siding	...	...	8 22	...	...	...	...	...	...	...	...
Dowlais Top	...	...	...	...	...	...	...	...	...	...	...
Dowlais	...	...	...	...	...	...	...	...	...	...	...
Pant	...	...	...	...	...	...	...	...	...	12 40	...
PONTSTICILL	...	...	...	...	...	...	...	...	...	...	...

STATIONS	C.B. Train		Goods and Empties		Rhymney Bran. Gds.		Thro' Goods.		C.B. Train.		G.W. Goods.		1st Trip A.M.		2nd Trip A.M.		3rd Trip P.M.		4th Trip P.M.	
	arr.	dep.	arr.	dep.	arr.	dep.	arr.	dep.	arr.	dep.	arr.	dep.	arr.	dep.	arr.	dep.	arr.	dep.	arr.	dep.
BASSALEG				2 20				2 40												
Rhiwderin																				
Church Road																				
Machen Line Kilns																				
Machen		1 10	2 40	2 50			3 0	3 10		3 50										
Machen Forge		1 20								4 0										
Rudry Sidings		1 30								4 15										
Caerphilly	1 40						3 20		4 40	4 30										
Bedwas				3 0				3 40												
Bryngwyn Siding																				
Maesycwmmer				3 20																
Maesycwmmer Junction																				
Fleur-de-lis			3 33	3 35		2 30						4 50								
Pengam			3 23			2 40						5 0								
Gilfach Colliery				3 45								5 10								
Gilfach Quarry																				
Aberbargoed Junction																				
Gwaelodywain Colliery																				
Lord Tredegar's Siding																				
Aberbargoed Station						3 0						5 20								
Elliot Pit				4								5 35								
Whiterose Colliery																				
Whiterose			4 10	4 20	3 5	3 10					5 45	6 10								
New Derlwyn Colliery																				
New Tredegar Pit			4 27	4 37	3 15	3 20						6 20								
McLaren No. 1			4 42			3 25														
RHYMNEY											6 25									
FLEUR-DE-LIS							3 45								9 15					
Pengam							4 0	4 5												
Bargoed Junction							4 15	4 20												
Darran Pit																				
Darran								4 35												
Deri Junction								4 45									12 20	12 30	3 7	
Fochriw								4 50							9 5			3 20	3 33	
Fochriw Pit Junction								5 0							9 22				3 43	
Pantywaen															9 40		12 40	12 50	3 53	
Rhymney I C. Siding								5 10							9 28	9 33	1 5		4 3	
Dowlais Top													6 40							
Dowlais													6 45			9 40	1 11		4 15	
Pant																				
PONTSTICILL								5 25					6 50			9 45		20	4 20	

NOTES.—1. If there are not sufficient Colliery Empties to make up a load for Nos. 1, 2 and 11 Up Trains, other traffic can be attached to form loads.

2. The Engine of 4.30 a.m. ex Bassaleg upon arrival at Rhymney will do all the shunting required at McLaren No. 1 and 2 Collieries, Buchan and Co's Shop Sidings, also White Rose Station Sidings, and MUST return to Rhymney in time to leave there PUNCTUALLY with 11.30 a.m. Minerals.

3. The 12.50 p.m. Rhymney Branch Minerals will do the work required at Collieries on the way down—put off their train at Fleur-de-lis and work back any traffic on hand at Fleur-de lis for Rhymney Branch at 2.30 p.m.

4. A Brakesman will join 6.15 a.m. Thro' Goods at Fleur-de-lis and assist Guard to Pantywaen, afterwards assist Guard of Pantywaen Train to Pontsticill and back, and work home to Fleur-de-lis with the 1.10 p.m. Thro' Goods ex Pantywaen.

5. The Machen and McLaren Collieries' Engines will, during the day run Special Trips, as and when required, between Bassaleg, Rhymney, and Pantywaen. Signalmen must give special attention to the working of these Engines, so that they may be available for working the Colliers' Trains to time each evening.

BETWEEN BASSALEG, RHYMNEY, & PONTSTICILL.

DOWN TRAINS.

Train columns:
1. 8.25 a.m. Minerals
2. 8.38 a.m. Bargoed Branch Gds & Min.
3. a.m. G.W. Goods
4. 10.45 a.m. Minerals
5. 11.30 a.m. Minerals
6. p.m. C.B. Train
7. p.m. G.W. Goods
8. 12.50 p.m. Rhymney Branch Minerals
9. 1.10 p.m. Thro' Goods
10. 1.35 p.m. Minerals
11. C.B. Train

STATIONS	1 arr	1 dep	2 arr	2 dep	3 arr	3 dep	4 arr	4 dep	5 arr	5 dep	6 arr	6 dep	7 arr	7 dep	8 arr	8 dep	9 arr	9 dep	10 arr	10 dep	11 arr	11 dep
PONTSTICILL																						
Pant						9 20																
Dowlais						9 32																
Dowlais Top						9 37																
Rhymney I.C. Siding																		1 10				
Pantywaen																						
Fochriw Pit Junct				8 38														1 35				
Fochriw				8 43														1 55				
Deri Junction			8 50	9 5																		
Darran																						
Darran Pit			9 20	9 32																		
Bargoed Junction			9 45	9 55													2 5	2 15				
Pengam																						
FLEUR-DE-LIS																						
RHYMNEY		8 25						10 45		11 30						12 50						
McLaren No. 1		8 35						10 55	11 35	12 5				12 50		1 0						
New Tredegar Pit		8 45						11 5		12 15						1 10						
New Derlwyn Colliery					9 42																	
Whiterose																						
Whiterose Colliery						9 50	11 10	11 20						12 58						1 35		
Elliot Pit	8 55	9 5				10 5		11 35	12 25	12 35			1 5	1 6		1 20			1 40	1 50		
Aberbargoed Station											12 25	12 40				1 33						
Lord Tredegar's Siding																						
Gwaelodywain Colliery																1 40						
Aberbargoed Junction		9 25		10 5	10 25	10 35		11 55		12 50				1 20		1 45		2 25		2 10		
Gilfach Quarry																						
Gilfach Colliery		9 35																				
Pengam							12 5	12 20	12 58	1 10						1 55						
Fleur-de-lls	9 43	9 53						12 33					1 24	1 30			2 30	2 45		2 23		
Maesycwmmer Junct													1 28	1 35								
Maesycwmmer		9 56								1 13								2 52		2 26		
Bryngwyn Siding																						
Bedwas		10 14						12 38										2 35		2 42		
Caerphilly																		2 45				1 55
Rhos Llantwit																						
Rudry Sidings																						
Machen Forge																						
Machen	10 23	10 33						12 46	1 35	1 45								3 18		2 52		2 10
Machen Lime Kilns																						
Church Road																						3 45
Rhiwderin																						
BASSALEG		10 53						1 35		2 5								3 45		3 15		3 40

Railway Working Timetable — Pontsticill / Rhymney to Bassaleg section

STATIONS	12 Guest Keen & Co's Col. Train (B Saturdays only) arr	dep	13 4.0 p.m. Rhymney Gds & Min. arr	dep	14 C.B. Train arr	dep	15 Guest Keen & Co's Col. Train (A Not on Saturdays) arr	dep	16 5.5 p.m. Minerals arr	dep	17 6.15 p.m. Thro' Goods arr	dep	18 G.W. Goods arr	dep	19 1st Trip A.M arr	dep	20 2nd Trip A.M arr	dep	21 3rd Trip P.M arr	dep	22 4th Trip P.M arr	dep
PONTSTICILL																						
Pant																7 35				2 0	2 50		4 30
Dowlais																7 45						4 10	
Dowlais Top															8 0	8 5	10 45	10 50				
Rhymney I.C. Siding																8 30					2 18		
Pantywaen		2 30						5 30							8 15	8 30	11 11				2 25		
Fochriw Pit Junction		2 35						5 36									11 15				2 40		
Fochriw		2 40						5 40								8 35	11 20					
Deri Junction		2 46						5 47														
Darran																	11 30	11 52				
Darran Pit																						
Bargoed Junction	2 53							5 55									12 5		2 54			
Penrann																						
FLEUR-DE-LIS																						
RHYMNEY				4 0						6 5	6 20	6 30										
McLaren No. 1			4 5																			
New Tredegar Pit				4 15					6 10	6 25				6 55								
New Derlwyn Colliery				4 23						6 35												
Whiterose																						
Whiterose Colliery				4 9						6 40				7 15								
Elliot Pit			4 40	4 33					6 45	6 55	6 38	6 43		7 20								
Aberbargoed Station											6 50	7 20										
Lord Tredegar's Siding																						
Gwa-llotywain Colliery																						
Aberbargoed Junction				5 10					7 15		7 30	7 0 7	7 34									
Gilfach Quarry																						
Gilfach Colliery																						
Pengam			5 20	5 25																		
Fleur-de-lis				5 28					7 25	7 40	7 41	7 39	7 44									
Maesycwmmer Junction												7 48	7 50									
Maesycwmmer					5 0	5 45				7 58	7 55	8 5										
Bryngwyn Siding				5 43	5 50	6 5			8 8	8 20	8 10	8 20										
Bedwas					5 15	6 15																
Caerphilly											8 48	8 55										
Rhos Llantwit																						
Rudry Sidings																						
Machen Forge																						
Machen			5 53																			
Machen Lime Kilns																						
Church Road									8 40		9 15											
Rhiwderin																						
BASSALEG			6 25																			

B Saturdays only.
A Not on Saturdays.

DOWN TRAINS.

BRECON A...

STATIONS.	TALYLLYN DAY GOODS. First Trip 1 a.m. arr	dep	Second Trip 2 a.m. arr	dep	Merthyr Branch Passengers 3 a.m. arr	dep	Merthyr Branch Goods 4 a.m. arr	dep	BRECON DAY GOODS First Trip 5 a.m. arr	dep	Second 6 p.m. arr
BRECON	...	...	...	...	...	...	...	...	...	8 10	...
Talyllyn	...	5 45	...	...	...	...	...	...	8 20	8 35	...
Talybont	...	6 0	...	...	...	...	...	...	8 45	8 55	12 50
Pentir-Rhiw	...	...	...	...	...	...	...	...	...	9 20	...
Torpantau	...	6 50	...	...	...	...	...	...	...	9 45	1 55
Dolygaer	...	...	...	...	...	...	...	...	...	...	...
Pontsticill	7 5	7 15	...	10 15	...	8 46	...	11 55	9 55	...	2 21
Morlais Junction	...	7 20	...	10 25	...	8 48	...	12 0	...	...	...
Pontsarn	...	...	...	...	...	*	...	...	...	...	...
Vaynor Siding	...	...	...	...	...	...	...	...	...	...	...
Cefn	...	7 35	10 40	10 50	8 55	8 56	12 15	12 34	...	...	...
Llwyncelyn Siding	...	7 44	..	10 59	...	...	...	12 43	...	...	...
Rhydycar Junction	...	7 49		11 4	...	9 5	12 48	...	...	...	...
MERTHYR, T.V.	7 51	...	11 10	...	...	...	12 55	1 5	...	...	3 37
Do. G.W.	...	...	...	...	9 7	...	1 10	...	...	...	3 39

UP TRAINS.

STATIONS.	TALYLLYN DAY GOODS. First Trip 1 a.m. arr	dep	Second Trip 2 a.m. arr	dep	Merthyr Branch Goods 3 a.m. arr	dep	Merthyr Branch Goods 4 p.m. arr	dep	BRECON DAY GOODS First Trip 5 a.m. arr	dep	Second 6 p.m. arr
MERTHYR, G.W.	...	...	...	...	...	9 50	...	1 20	...	...	...
Do. T.V.	...	8 30	...	11 40	...	..	...	...	...	...	4 5
Rhydycar Junction	...	8 32	...	11 42	...	10 26	...	1 22	...	...	...
Llwyncelyn Siding	...	8 35	...	12 25	...	10 35	...	1 30	...	...	...
Cefn	...	8 55	12 33	12 45	10 40	11 0	...	1 36	...	...	...
Vaynor Siding	...	...	...	...	...	...	...	...	...	...	...
Pontsarn	...	...	...	...	...	...	...	...	...	...	...
Morlais Junction	...	9 4	...	1 5	...	11 8	...	1 45	...	...	...
Pontsticill	9 9	...	1 11	2 5	11 14	...	1 55	3 35	...	10 20	5 5
Dolygaer	...	...	...	...	...	...	...	...	...	...	...
Torpantau	...	...	...	2 15	...	...	...	3 45	...	10 35	...
Pentir-Rhiw	...	...	2 40	2 50	...	...	...	4 10	...	11 0	...
Talybont	...	...	...	3 15	...	...	...	4 36	...	11 25	...
Talyllyn	...	...	3 25	...	...	...	4 50	...	11 40	...	7 2
BRECON	...	...	...	...	...	...	...	...	...	...	7 30

NOTES.

TALYLLYN DAY GOODS.

1. To be worked by two Talyllyn Engines.

2. Upon arrival at Pontsticill, one Engine will take up the working of Nos. 1 and 2 Down and Up Trips, and the other Engine to work Nos. 3 and 4 Down and Up Trips, also 2.50 p m. Passenger Train ex Merthyr as required.

3. No. 2 Up Trip worked by Talyllyn Engine, will leave Pontsticill 2.5 p.m. and work home to Talyllyn with a single Engine Load.

4. The Second Engine will leave Pontsticill 3.35 p.m. with a Train of Goods for Talyllyn.

TALYLLYN NIGHT GOODS				GOODS TRAIN, MONDAYS ONLY, R.R.				BRECON SHUNTER.					
First Trip		Second Trip		First Trip		Second Trip		First Trip		Second Trip		Third Trip	
7		8		9		10						R. R.	
p.m.		a.m.		a.m.		a.m.		a.m.		a.m.		p.m.	
arr	dep	arr	dep	arr	dep	arr	dep	arr	dep	arr	dep	arr	dep
...	6 20	...	...	...	3 25	...	...	...	6 20	...	11 40	...	4 25
6 30	6 40	...	12 30	3 35	3 40	...	...	6 30	...	11 55	...	4 35	...
6 50	7 0	12 40	12 45	...	3 55	...	...	...	...	...	...	...	...
...	7 25	...	1 10	...	4 20	...	...	...	...	...	...	...	...
7 48	7 50	...	1 35	...	4 45	...	...	...	...	...	...	...	...
...	...	...	...	...	...	...	...	...	...	...	...	...	...
...	8 15	1 50	...	5 0	5 15	...	8 0	...	...	...	...	...	...
...	8 31	...	...	...	5 25	...	8 10	...	...	...	...	...	...
...	...	...	...	...	...	...	...	...	...	...	...	...	...
...	8 45	...	...	...	5 40	...	8 25	...	...	...	...	...	...
...	8 55	...	...	...	5 47	...	8 35	...	...	...	...	...	...
...	9 0	...	...	...	5 52	...	8 40	...	...	...	...	...	...
9 5	...	...	...	5 55	...	8 45	...	...	...	...	...	...	...
...	...	...	...	...	...	...	...	...	...	...	...	...	...

UP TRAINS.

TALYLLYN NIGHT GOODS				GOODS TRAIN, MONDAYS ONLY, R.R.				BRECON SHUNTER.					
First Trip		Second Trip		First Trip		Second Trip		First Trip		Second Trip		Third Trip	
7		8		9		10							
p.m.		a.m.		a.m.		a.m.		a.m.		p.m.		p.m.	
arr	dep	arr	dep	arr	dep	arr	dep	arr	dep	arr	dep	arr	dep
...	9 35	...	...	...	6 58	...	9 45	...	...	...	...	...	...
...	9 37	...	...	...	7 0	...	9 47	...	...	...	...	...	...
...	...	...	...	...	...	...	9 52	...	...	...	...	...	...
9 47	9 50	...	...	...	7 12	10 0	10 18	...	...	...	...	...	...
...	...	...	...	...	...	...	...	...	...	...	...	...	...
...	10 0	...	...	...	7 20	...	10 25	...	...	...	...	...	...
10 10	10 30	...	2 30	7 30	...	10 30	11 10	...	...	...	...	...	...
...	10 45	...	2 45	...	...	...	11 25	...	...	...	...	...	...
...	11 10	...	3 10	...	...	...	11 50	...	...	...	...	...	...
...	11 35	...	3 35	...	...	...	12 15	...	...	...	...	...	...
11 50	...	3 50	4 †15	...	...	12 30	1 40	...	9 5	...	12 30	...	4 55
...	...	4†15	...	...	...	1 48	...	9 20	...	12 40	...	5 5	...

TALYLLYN NIGHT GOODS.

1.   Brecon Engine, which assists in working this train from Talyllyn, to leave Brecon light at 6.20 p.m.

2.   † Brecon Light Engine.

SPECIAL NOTICE.—All Goods Trains from Torpantau to Talybont must be brought to a stop at North End of Torpantau Tunnel for brakes to be put down, and Guard in charge of train must also ring the Bell Communication to Torpantau Station

WORKING TIME TABLE FOR

UP TRAINS.

STATIONS.	1		2		3		4		5	
	McLaren Colliers' Train		McLaren Colliers' Train S & M E		McLaren Empty Carr. S & M E		McLaren Colliers' Train S & M O		McLaren Empty Carr. S & M O	
	a.m.		p.m.		p.m.		p m.		p.m.	
	arr	dep	arr	dep	arr	dep	arr	dep	arr	dep
Maesycwmmer ...	...	6 0	...	...	...	6 15	...	...	...	3 25
Fleur-de-lis ...	...	...	...	4 25	6 20	...	...	1 50	3 35	...
Pengam ...	...	6 5	...	4 45	...	...	...	2 0	...	...
Aberbargoed Junction...	...	6 8	...	...	...	...	...	...	...	...
Aberbargoed Station ...	...	6 11	...	...	...	...	...	...	...	...
Elliot Pit Junction Box	...	6 16	...	...	...	...	...	...	...	...
White Rose ...	...	6 20	...	5 15	...	...	...	2 15	...	...
McLaren No. 1 ...	...	6 25	5 20	5 25	...	...	...	2 25	...	...
Rhymney ...	6 28	...	5 29	...	...	...	2 30	...	...	...

NOTES & SPECIAL

S & M E—Does not run on Saturdays nor Mondays.

S & M O—Runs on Saturdays and Mondays only.

† Empty Train from McLaren No. 1 to Fleur-de-lis, but, if any night-men returning home to Maesycwmmer in this Train, it must run on to Maesycwmmer.

1. These Colliers' Trains must stop at Pengam, Aberbargoed Junction Platform, Aberbargoed Station, and White Rose, to pick up and set down Colliers to and from McLaren No. 1 Colliery.

2. One of McLaren Colliers' Coaches will be attached to 6.0 p.m. Passengers *ex* Rhymney to Maesycwmmer and back daily to convey Night-men up from Maesycwmmer to Colliery.

3. These Colliers' Trains to be worked by the Fleur-de-lis Engine and men. Guard Wm. Thomas.

4. After running the first Up and Down Colliers' Trains, this Engine and men to work as required during the day, but must be ready to leave Fleur-de-lis punctually each day as shewn in the Time Table, to work the last Up and Down McLaren Colliers' Train.

5. These Colliers' Trains must be run punctually at the times shewn. Goods and Mineral Trains must be kept clear.

6. The McLaren Colliers' Coaches will stand at Fleur-de-lis when not in use.

7. Guard Wm. Thomas must see that hand brake of van is properly screwed down before the Engine is cut off.

McLAREN COLLIERS' TRAINS.

DOWN TRAINS.

STATIONS.	1 McLaren Empty Carr.		2 McLaren Colliers' Train		3 McLaren Colliers' Train S & M E		4 McLaren Colliers' Train S & M O	
	arr a.m.	dep	arr a.m.	dep	arr p.m.	dep	arr p.m.	dep
Rhymney ...	...	...	...	6 36	...	5 40	...	2 45
McLaren No. 1 ...	...	...	...	6 45	...	5 47	...	2 52
White Rose ...	...	...	...	6 49	...	5 50	...	2 55
Elliot Pit Junction Box	...	...	...	6 52	...	5 53	...	2 58
Aberbargoed Station ...	...	...	...	6 57	...	5 57	...	3 2
Aberbargoed Junction...	...	...	...	6 59	...	6 0	...	3 5
Pengam ...	...	...	...	7 2	...	6 4	...	3 9
Fleur-de-lis ...	...	5 50	†7 7	...	...	...	...	...
Maesycwmmer ...	5 55	...	...	...	6 10	...	3 15	...

INSTRUCTIONS.

8. Each workman should be supplied with a metal check (numbered) by the Tredegar Iron and Coal Company, and this check must be carried by workmen when Travelling by the Trains, and shewn whenever required. A strict examination must be made daily of these Workmen's Trains to see that the men travelling are each provided with the proper check. If any man be found travelling without a check his name and address must be at once obtained, at what pit or place employed, and occupation. The result of these examinations to be given on Agent's Daily Report Form.

9. Agents to keep a correct daily record in the Train Book of the number of men travelling by these Trains to and from their Stations.

10. Care must be taken to prevent the workmen getting in and out of the carriages whilst the Train is in motion, and any case of disobedience to be reported, giving name of Collier and number of his check.

11. Care must also be taken to see that all the carriage doors of these Colliers' Trains are properly shut and fastened before starting away from platforms

12. A Colliers' Platform is erected opposite McLaren No. 1 Colliery for the use of the Colliers to and from that Colliery, and Guard of Train must see that no workman is allowed to get in or leave the train except at this platform.

13. The following Signal Boxes to be opened at times shewn hereunder :—

SIGNAL BOX.			A.M.
Maesycwmmer Station	...	...	5.45
Fluer-de-lis ...	...	...	5.45
Aberbargoed Junction	...	...	6.0
Elliot Pit Junction	...	...	6.5
White Rose Station	...	...	6.15
McLaren No. 1 ...	...	...	6.18
Rhymney Station ...	...	...	6.23

WORKING

POWELL DUFFRYN COMPANY'S

UP TRAINS.

STATIONS.	1 Machen Colliers' Train.		2 Machen Colliers' Empty Carriages Mondays and Saturdays only.		3 Machen Colliers' Empty Carriages Mondays and Saturdays excepted.	
	a.m. arr	dep	p.m. arr	dep	p.m. arr	dep
Bassaleg ...	...	5*30	...	...	...	...
Machen ...	5*42	5 55	...	...	...	...
Bedwas ...	...	6 2	...	...	...	...
Maesycwmmer ...	...	6 11	...	...	...	...
Maesycwmmer Junction...	...	...	...	...	...	...
Fleur-de-lis	...	...	...	...	...	...
Pengam ...	...	6 16	...	...	...	...
Aberbargoed Junction ...	...	6 21	...	...	...	...
Aberbargoed Station ...	...	6 26	...	...	...	...
Coedymoeth Pit ...	...	6 31	...	...	...	...
Elliot Pit ...	...	6 35	...	...	...	...
Whiterose ...	...	6 40	...	2 15	...	5 20
New Tredegar Colliery ...	6 45	...	2 20	...	5 23	...

NOTES & SPECIAL

* Light Engine.

The Engine for working the Machen Colliers' Train will leave Bassaleg light at 5.30 a.m This Engine after working No. 3 Down Colliers' Train to Machen must be given every facility for returning home to Bassaleg in the evening, so as not to delay it unnecessarily.

The 5.55 a.m. Colliers' Train from Machen will be extended from Whiterose Station to McLaren No. 1 Box for the purpose of taking up P.D. Colliers to New Tredegar Colliery returning at once to Whiterose with the empty carriages . Engine will afterwards work Goods Traffic as required during the day and must be ready to work Colliers' Trains in the evening.

On Tuesdays, Wednesdays, Thursdays, and Fridays, the carriages will be pushed up in front of Engine from Whiterose to New Tredegar Colliery Platform under the Short Section Block and start from New Tredegar Colliery at 5.25 p.m

On Mondays and Saturdays, the Machen Colliers' Empty Coaches will run from Whiterose to McLaren No. 1 attached to the McLaren Colliers' Train and return at once, picking up P.D. Colliers at New Tredegar Pit at 2.25 p.m.

These Colliers' Trains must be run punctually at the times shewn. Goods and Mineral Trains must be kept clear.

The 6.31 p.m. Rhymney Branch Passenger Train ex Maesycwmmer will convey Colliers to Elliot Pit, and two or more Colliers' Carriages are attached to this Train for that purpose.

Care must be taken to prevent the workmen getting in and out of the Carriages whilst the Train is in motion, and any case of disobedience to be reported, giving name of Collier and number of his check.

TIME TABLE

MACHEN COLLIERS' TRAINS.

DOWN TRAINS.

STATIONS.	1 Machen Colliers' Empty Carriages.		2 Machen Colliers' Train. Mondays and Saturdays only.		3 Machen Colliers' Train. Mondays and Saturdays excepted.	
	a.m.		p.m.		p.m.	
	arr	dep	arr	dep	arr	dep
New Tredegar Colliery ...	...	6 50	...	2 25	...	5 25
White Rose ...	6 55	...	...	...	...	...
Elliot Pit ...		...	...	2 35	...	5 30
Coedymoeth Pit ...	...	...	...	2 38	...	5 33
Aberbargoed Station ...	...	...	...	2 42	...	5 37
Aberbargoed Junction ...	...	...	...	2 45	...	5 39
Pengam ...	...	...	...	2 50	...	5 44
Fluer-de-lis ...	...	...	...	...	...	...
Maesycwmmer ...	...	...	...	2 55	...	5 49
Bedwas ...	...	...	...	3 5	...	5 59
Machen ...	...	...	3 12	3*18	6 6	6*12
Bassaleg ...	...	...	3*28	...	6*22	...

INSTRUCTIONS.

Care must also be taken to see that all the Carriage doors of the Workmen's Trains are properly shut and fastened before starting away from platforms.

Each workman should be supplied with a metal check (numbered) by the Powell Duffryn Coal Company, and this check must be carried by workmen when travelling by the Trains, and shewn whenever required. A strict examination must be made daily of these Workmen's Trains to see that the men travelling are each provided with the proper check. If any man be found travelling without a check his name and address must be at once obtained, at what pit or place employed, and occupation. The result of these examinations to be given on Agents Daily Report Form.

Agents to keep a correct daily record in the Train Book of the number of men travelling by these Trains to and from their Stations.

Platforms have been erected for the use of workmen travelling by these Trains at :—

NEW TREDEGAR COLLIERY   } These platforms will be lighted at
ELLIOT PIT   night by Powell Duffryn Co.
COEDYMOETH PIT

ABERBARGOED JUNCTION   } Lamps to be lighted by Aberbargoed Junction Signalman.

In order to avoid coming in contact with these Colliers' Platforms, Goods and Mineral Guards and Brakesmen when working Trains past them must be careful not to leave their Vans.

Appendix Three

Opening and Closing of Stations

MAIN LINE

	Opened	Closed to passengers	Closed to goods
Brecon (Free Street)	1. 3.1871	31.12.1962	None
†Brecon (Watton)	23. 4.1863	31.12.1871	4. 5.1964
Groesffordd Halt	c.1932	31.12.1962	None
†Brynderwen	23. 4.1863	30. 9.1869	None
Talyllyn Jn	1.10.1869	31.12.1962	31.12.1962
†Talybont	19. 3.1863	31.12.1962	1. 7.1963
Pentir Rhiw	1909	31.12.1962	None
Torpantau	c.1870	31.12.1962	1959
Pontsticill Jn	1. 8.1867	31.12.1962	31.12.1962
Pant (second)	5.1869	31.12.1962	31.12.1962
Dowlais Top	1. 9 1868	31.12.1962	27. 3.1961
Pantywaun Halt	c.1920	31.12.1962	31.12.1962
Fochriew	13. 9.1868	31.12.1962	31.12.1962
Ogilvie Village H.	c.1920	31.12.1962	None
(Darran & Deri RR)	31. 3.1858		
(Bargoed RR)	31. 3.1858		
Pengam (Mon.)	14. 6.1865	31.12.1962	31.12.1962*
Fleur-de-Lis Halt	1926	31.12.1962	None
Maesycwmmer	14. 6.1865	31.12.1962	31.12.1962
Bedwas	14. 6.1865	31.12.1962	16. 7.1964*
Trethomas	1915	31.12.1962	16. 7.1964*
Machen	14. 6.1865	31.12.1962	16. 7.1964*
Church Road	14. 6.1865	16. 9.1957	16. 9.1957
Rhiwderin	14. 6.1865	1. 3.1954	14. 9.1959
Bassaleg	14. 6.1865	31.12.1962	16. 7.1964*

† Official opening 1st May
* Remain in use for bulk freight

DOWLAIS BRANCH

	Opened	Closed to passengers	Closed to goods
Pant (first)	19. 3.1863	5.1869	None
Pantyscallog Halt	6.1911	2. 5.1960(a)	None
Dowlais Central	23. 6.1869	2. 5.1960(a)	22.11.1954

MERTHYR BRANCH

	Opened	Closed to passengers	Closed to goods
Pont Sarn	c.1900	13.11.1961	
Cefn Coed	1. 8.1867	13.11.1961	None
Heolgerrig Halt	31. 5.1937	13.11.1961	None
(Merthyr High Street, GW)	1. 8 1868	27.11.1967(b)	27.11.1967

(a) Workmen only; closed to public 28.6.1952
(b) B&M service ceased 13.11.1961

RHYMNEY BRANCH

	Opened	Closed to passengers	Closed to goods
Aberbargoed Jn Platform	c.1900	31.12.1962	None
Aberbargoed & Bargoed	1800	31.12.1962	7.1953
Cwmsyfiog (first)	1908	5. 7.1937	None
Cwmsyfiog (second)	5. 7.1937	31.12.1962	None
Elliot Pit Halt	c.1900	31.12.1962	None
New Tredegar	c.1866	31.12.1962	31.12.1962
Abertysswg	1905	14. 4.1930(c)	None
Rhymney B&M	16. 4.1866	14. 4.1930(c)	14. 4.1930(d)

(c) Last train four days earlier
(d) Continued in use as siding via ex-Rhymney Railway branch from Tir Phil

CAERPHILLY BRANCH (e)

	Opened	Closed to passengers	Closed to goods
White Hart Halt	1947	30. 6.1952	None
Waterloo Halt	1904	15. 9.1956	None
Fountain Bridge Halt	1904	15. 9.1956	None
Gwernydomen Halt	1904	15. 9.1956	None

(e) Branch opened for goods 1864: for passengers 28.12.1887 but without station on B&M section.

Authorities

E.A. Pratt, *British Railways and the Great War* (Selwyn & Blount, 1921).

E.T. MacDermot, *History of the Great Western Railway* (GWR, 1927 and 1931).

G.P. Neele, *Railway Reminiscences* (McCorquodale, 1904).

Clement E. Stretton, *The History of the Midland Railway* (Methuen, 1901).

C.S. Howells, *Transport Facilities in South Wales and Monmouthshire* (University College, Cardiff, 1911).

R.J. Rimell, Davies, and Hailey, *History of the Barry Railway Company, 1884–1921* (Western Mail, Cardiff, 1923).

D.S. Barrie and Charles E. Lee, *The Sirhowy Valley and its Railways* (Railway Publishing Co., 1940).

D.S. Barrie, *The Taff Vale Railway* (The Oakwood Press, 2nd Edn, 1950), and *The Rhymney Railway* (The Oakwood Press, 1952).

V.J. Parry, *Brecon & Merthyr Railway* (Privately, 1970).

The Railway Magazine, especially XLIII (1918), 73 (H.L. Hopwood), and LI (1922), 20 and 110 :E.L. Ahrons).

Herapath's Journal; The Engineer.

GWR Magazine (XXXIV (1922), 495).

Locomotive, Carriage & Wagon Review (XXXVII (1931)).

Railway Review (series by W.H. Perrin, 1950).

Bradshaw's Guide; Bradshaw's Railway Manual; Brecon & Radnor Express; Star of Gwent; Cardiff & Merthyr Guardian; Merthyr Telegraph.

MERTAYR

Merthyr tramcars at a passing loop; these formed an integral transport system, with
the railway, for the town of Merthyr.   *R.W. Rush*

A 1922 view of a typical local service train with No. 17, 0−6−0ST on the 3.5 pm
Dowlais to Pant service seen here in August 1922 at Ivor Junction.
                                            L.C.G.B., Ken Nunn Collection

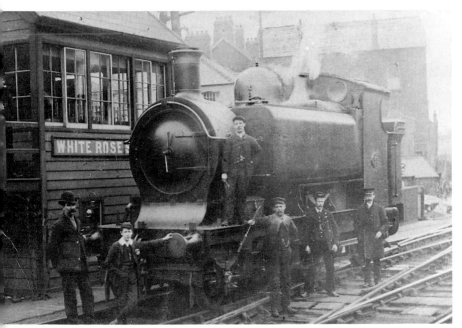

This outside-framed 4–4–0PT, B&M No. 35, had been GWr 1490, built 1898, then sold to the Ebbw Vale Steel Co. The B&M purchased it in 1908, but sold it on in 1916 to the Cramlington Coal Co. Its bogie was fitted with wooden Mansell wheels, it was mainly used on the Rhymney branch and is seen here at New Tredegar, formerly called White Rose.   *R.C. Riley Collection*

Index

Aberbargoed Junction 9, 110, 113, 131
Accidents 8, 59, 61, 131
Alexandra Docks & Railway Co. 43–4, 47, 52, 110

B&A Rly 13
Banks, W.L. 22
Bargoed–Rhymney Valley 31, 33, 37, 44, 111
Bargoed–Taff Valley 38
Bargoed South Junction 9, 93
Barry Railway 9, 44–5, 58, 110
Brecon Mountain Railway 139, 141
Brecknock & Abergavenny Canal 13, 15, 23, 91
Bryn Oer Tramroad 15, 93

Cambrian Railways 52, 57–8, 66, 68, 88, 132
Carriages 85, 88
Central Wales Railway 14, 22, 49
Cobb, J. 13–4, 22
Colliers' Platforms 54, 113
Colliers' Trains 54, 88, 113
Conybeare, H. 13–4, 19, 22, 25, 30, 45

Cyfartha Castle 25, 31
Cyfartha Ironworks 19, 26, 110–1

Davies, David 16, 18, 48
Deri Junction 9, 37–8, 44, 47, 93
de Winton, J.P. 13, 22, 47
Duffryn Isaf 44

Ebbw Vale & Cardiff Junction Railway 45
Elliot Collieries 35, 113, 137

Glyn Collwyn 93
Gradients 92
Guest, Sir John 13
GWR 7, 25, 35, 38, 41, 43–5, 48, 50, 52, 74, 78, 85, 88, 93, 110–1, 131–2, 134

Hay Tramroad 14–6
Henshaw, A. 43, 47
Heol Lladron (Brecon Junction) 27, 91
HH&B Rly 15–6, 19, 22–3, 26, 66, 68, 85

Ivor Junction 26, 39, 139
Ivor Works 26

Llangorse Lake   91
Llwyn Celyn Junction   26, 111
LNWR   7, 13–4, 31, 33, 37, 39, 41, 45, 47, 49,
     93, 110
Locomotives   18–9, 59, 61, 63–83, 131–2,
     134, 141
Locomotive Superintendents   61, 63, 74

Machen Loop Line   44, 113
Machen Works   9, 47, 61, 63, 74, 78
Maerdy Colliery   35, 113
Maes y Cwmmer Junction   35, 110
Manchester & Milford Railway   52, 85
McLaren Collieries   35, 113, 137
Midland Railway   7, 23, 27, 30, 35, 41, 45, 58,
     73, 85
Mid-Wales Railway   8, 14–6, 19, 22–3, 27,
     30, 49, 52
Monmouthshire Railway   23, 35, 41, 50
Morlais Junction   39, 41, 49
MT&A Rly   13, 33, 37, 41

NA&H Rly   9, 35, 61, 85
Neath & Brecon Railway   22, 27, 30, 41, 45,
     66, 73
New Tredegar Colliery   35
Nine Mile Point   33, 45, 47

Old Rumney   8–9, 14, 33, 35, 38, 43–4, 54,
     61, 63, 113, 137
Owen, G.C.   63

Pantywaun Tramway   93
Park Mile   43, 110
PC&N Rly   43–4, 88, 139
Pentwyn Reservoir   19
Penywern Junction   26, 39
Pontsticill Junction   9

Rhos Llantwit Colliery   113
Rhydycar Junction   26, 41, 49, 111
Rhymney Ironworks   14–5, 33, 113
Rhymney Limestone Railway   11, 37, 93
Rhymney Railway   7–9, 14, 25, 31, 33, 35,
     37–8, 43–5, 47, 50, 52, 54, 58, 61, 93,
     110–1, 113, 131–2, 137
Rising Sun Deviation   35

Savin, T.   18–9, 22–3, 25, 66, 68, 85
Seven Mile Bank   8–9, 14, 18, 23, 45, 49, 59,
     91
Simpson, J.T.   61, 63
Sirhowy Railway   33, 41
Stations (B&M):
   Aberbargoed   111–2
   Abertysswg   113
   Bassaleg   8–9, 110
   Bedwas   110
   Brecon Free St   26–7, 30, 91, 139

Brecon Mount St   27, 30
Brecon Watton   19, 27, 30, 91, 134, 139
Brithdir   59
Brynerwen   19, 30
Cefn Coed   110
Church Road   110, 136
Dolygaer   19, 93
Dowlais Central   111, 139
Dowlais Top   26, 39, 93
Fleur-de-Lis   37, 110
Fochriew   93
Fountain Bridge Halt   44, 113, 139
Groesffordd Halt   91
Gwernydomen Halt   113
Heolgerrig Halt   111
Machen   110, 113, 139
Maesycwmmer   54, 110
Merthyr   25, 41, 57, 61, 111
New Tredegar   113, 131, 139
Ogilvie Village Halt   93
Pant   18, 25–6, 93, 139
Pantyscallog   26, 136
Pantywaen Halt   93
Pengam   37, 110
Pentir Rhiw   19, 91, 139
Pont Sarn   8, 110
Pontsticill   57, 93, 139
Rhiwderin   110, 136, 139
Rhymney Lower   37, 113, 131, 139
Talybont   18–9, 23, 59, 61, 91, 134, 139
Talyllyn   19, 22, 30, 52, 91, 131
Torpantau   19, 93, 131, 139
Trethomas   110, 139
Waterloo Halt   44, 113
White Hart Halt   44, 113, 139
White Rose   35, 113
Steam Railcars (AD&R)   52
Summit Tunnel   9
Sutherland, A.   18, 25

Taff Vale Railway   7, 13, 19, 25, 31, 33, 37–8,
     43, 52, 57, 111
Talyllyn Junction   9, 16, 91
Talyllyn Tunnel   16, 18, 30, 134, 136, 139
Torpantau Tunnel   16, 18, 137
Trehir Quarry   57, 110
Trevil Quarries   15, 93
Twynnau Gwvnnion Quarries   11, 93

Usk Valley Railway Co.   41

Vale of Crickhowell Railway   41
Vale of Neath Railway   25–6
Vaynor Quarries   110, 137

Watkin, Sir Edward   45

Ynysfach Ironworks   26
Ynysfach Junction   111